SPIRITED STONE

LESSONS FROM KUBOTA'S GARDEN

SPIRITED STONE

LESSONS FROM KUBOTA'S GARDEN

photography by

GEMINA GARLAND-LEWIS

CHIN MUSIC PRESS

CHIN MUSIC
P R E S S

Published by:
Chin Music Press
1501 Pike Place #329
Seattle, WA 98101
USA

WWW.CHINMUSICPRESS.COM

Publication of this book has been supported by generous grants from the Stanley Smith Horticultural Trust; the Pendleton and Elisabeth Carey Miller Charitable Foundation; Furthermore: a program of the J.M. Kaplan Fund; David R. Coffin Grant from Foundation for Landscape Studies; 4Culture; and Robert Chinn Foundation.

Furthermore:
a program of the J.M. Kaplan Fund

First [1] edition

Cover photography: Gemina Garland-Lewis
Book design: Dan D Shafer & Carla Girard
Cover design and book layout: Dan D Shafer

Printed in Canada

Library of Congress Cataloging in Publication Data available upon request.

ISBN: 978-1-63405-975-6

The cover photo features the Fossil Stone at the juncture of the main path and the Moon Bridge. The fossils embedded in the stone are about forty million years old. The fossilized horsetails were sixty feet high back then, and the coast began at present-day Issaquah. A friend of Fujitarō Kubota's who managed a stone quarry gave him the stone around 1967.

While we are here, we do what we can. Then the next generation comes along and does what they can. There is more to do and, if we strive for it, we will get it done.

TOM KUBOTA

Table of Contents

Foreword

Charles Johnson

KUBOTA GARDEN IS A MAGNIFICENT work of art. I'm not the least bit hesitant to call it a masterpiece of both Shintoism and the Buddha Dharma, and to add that those who walk through its twenty acres in south Seattle discover that during their visit they, too, become part of its natural beauty, tranquility, and spirit of place.

Recently, a dear Buddhist friend and I toured the ninety-two-year-old Garden. In 2007, I took my vows (the Precepts) in the Soto Zen tradition. She has taken refuge in a Tibetan lineage. We are both black Americans. And this trip was our Pacific Northwest version of what the Japanese call *shinrin-yoku* or "forest bathing."

Walking the many forested paths of gravel and stone, we both sensed the healing benefits of such an oxygen-rich environment, but also the impossibility of ever truly capturing what we were experiencing in something as limited as language, though we both are long-time workers with words. For this well-kept Garden is, first and foremost and finally, an abundant feast for all one's senses. And especially for our bodies that must negotiate stretches of forest, descend hills on steps of rock, and cross a Moon Bridge that is intentionally "Difficult to walk up and hard to walk down." Here, the Earth, so pure and primordial, delivers a dualism-transcending spirit tabernacled in the diverse forms of nature. Here, Earth's ecology appears in its most elemental guise as the solidity and timelessness of fossil stone forty million years old, in the vastness of sky, the formlessness of water, the gift of trees, moss, lawns and late summer blooming plants, and open spaces—emptiness or *śūnyatā*—all so delicately interwoven and interdependent in an elegant simplicity. And we felt how we were naturally woven into this constantly changing tapestry, though urban life too often makes us forgetful of this, our original face.

So this is a poetic landscape for refuge and meditation, a work of art we could walk within that awakened in us a feeling of serenity, humility, and gratitude. A place that beckoned us to forget all our quotidian cares as city dwellers, to slow down the hectic pace of modern life and listen quietly and viscerally with our spirit and flesh. Like all things impermanent, we are from this place and one day will return to it—to nourish it as it nourished us now. (In one sense, then, we never die, the Garden told us. And all that has ever been is still present around us.) It invited us to feel and know that we *are* the rugged texture of tree bark, the gentle sound of water rippling over stones, and the shimmer of sunlight on a koi pond fed by underground springs. I couldn't help but recall a Sanskrit line, *Tat tvam asi,* "You are that," when my form merged with the stone benches for meditation, and when I realized how the individual stone sculptures gracefully placed along the Way I walked each had its own character, personality and *haecceitas* or "thisness," to borrow a term from medieval philosopher Duns Scotus.

At Kubota Garden, the paths forked often, seducing me to try this direction, then that one, and all drew me from one aesthetic wonder to another. Our spiritually renewing forest bath among Japanese maples and threadleaf cypresses led us from the red-railed Heart Bridge to a Necklace of Ponds, from there to the Tom Kubota Stroll Garden and the Kasuga Lantern in the Japanese Garden. On and on, at every turn and corner, this remarkable public park that makes you feel you might be in Japan and not Seattle (though both enjoy similarities in natural splendor), nudged us to the Waterfall at the Mountainside, through the Fera Fera Forest, and to the Terrace Overlook.

While words fail this writer to capture the beauty of Kubota Garden, the contributors to *Spirited Stone* do, in fact, achieve in their fine essays, poems, interviews, and photography an appreciation, an homage, to the vision of master gardener Fujitarō Kubota and his family members who created, expanded, and preserved this treasure for us all. But, no. Words are merely "a finger pointing at the moon," and cannot be a substitute for experiencing firsthand all that the Garden offers.

Go there.

Introduction

Thaïsa Way

IT IS NOT SURPRISING that Seattle and the Pacific Northwest boast some of the finest Japanese gardens in the United States.[1] Located on the Pacific Rim, just an ocean away from Japan, the landscape is not dissimilar with its snow-capped mountains, towering forests, and dramatic water views. The Japanese garden seems regionally appropriate. And indeed, over a century of Japanese immigration and development, the role of Japanese arts and culture has grown to become an integral part of what is recognized as Pacific Northwest character. Kubota Garden is a part of this legacy, offering its own unique narrative of what it means to create and steward a garden in the Pacific Northwest.

Kubota Garden was designed and built by a Japanese American nurseryman and garden designer, Fujitarō Kubota. From 1927, when he purchased the land, till his death in 1973, when his son Tom Kubota took leadership over the garden, Kubota crafted a landscape that has come to embody one of the many immigrant experiences of our region. Kubota's legacy is extensive, as his designs and the plants grown in his nursery are to be found in hundreds of gardens and landscapes in and around Seattle, including Bloedel Reserve on Bainbridge Island. His twenty-acre garden, as Betsy Anderson observes in her essay (see page 189), while not a humble landscape, is nonetheless one of our most remarkable models of a Pacific Northwest vernacular and cultural landscape.

Kubota Garden is simultaneously American and Japanese, a unique place of its own here in Seattle. Kubota drew inspiration from the plants, stones, and waters of the region in accordance with the natural character of his new home. Then through the lens of his Japanese culture, he created an extraordinary landscape and business that in turn shaped the region's landscapes and public realm. As such, Kubota Garden is more than just the legacy of one Japanese immigrant to the United States. It is a gardener's garden and a nurseryman's landscape. It is a cultural landscape layered with narratives of immigration, labor, conflict, idealism, translation, and resilience. It is also a landscape that is about the aspirations of democracy, of a country that in its best moments has embraced immigrants and expanded its imagination to engage new inscriptions on the landscape and in the public realm. It is for this reason essential that this book is a layered and poetic exploration of the experience of the garden, through the eyes, ears, and hands of gardeners, nurserymen, colleagues, and family, and the community stewards of the garden as well as artists, poets, and scholars.

This collection makes visible the optimism with which Kubota built the garden and then, after being incarcerated during World War II, rebuilt the garden at an even greater scale. It echoes the garden as each contribution shapes a unique portal on the garden. It is meant to arouse the imagination and offer a narrative of making places that are enduring and real. It is a collection of essays, interviews, and poems, commissioned especially for this project, offering a rich and textured experience enhancing that of visiting the garden on any given day.

To create a garden is to make a special place. It is often one of the first acts of newcomers and immigrants; to make a home on the land. Gardening, as Jeff Hou describes in his essay (see page 31), is a "humble act of recreation, an expression of one's culture and identity, or as a means of making a living, was an activity that many people, immigrants or not, have experienced." In the case of Kubota Garden, the land became the cultural inscription for the community of Japanese Americans and others in the decades of its development and stewardship in South Seattle. It was not an easy narrative as the community has faced not only the challenges of immigration, but the deep-seated resentments of some that have at times taken the form of alien land laws, exclusionary regulations, and in its worst moments, wartime incarceration. Kubota Garden comes to signify the strength and resilience associated with garden-making and putting down roots, and then surviving not only the challenges of racism and exclusion but development pressure and other economic changes far beyond the garden itself. These are the layers that compose Kubota Garden, creating what Hou describes as "a place of survival and livelihood, a place of social gathering and community building, and a place of adaptation and resilience."

Fujitarō Kubota (1880–1973) immigrated to the United States and by 1907 had joined the three-thousand-plus Issei (first-generation Japanese immigrants) in Washington, at the heart of the Pacific Northwest. In the midst of a recession, Kubota formed the Kubota Gardening Company. Within a few years, Kubota had purchased five acres of a logged marsh landscape on Renton Avenue South in south Seattle. Despite the thick brush, he was taken by the rolling topography, the natural springs, and a perennial creek.[2] Hiring a caretaker, Kubota drained and dried the wetland, cut trails, dug ponds, built bridges, and planted an extensive collection of trees and shrubs, traditional Japanese plants as well as those common in the Pacific Northwest. This was the beginning of a stroll garden grounded in the ecology of the Pacific Northwest.

The landscape of Kubota Garden reveals Kubota's design language, suggesting an alternative translation of Japanese aesthetics in the Seattle region, one as much a part of the Pacific Northwest landscape as it is Japanese. He never drew his designs on paper but rather asked clients to select from the diverse array of garden vignettes displayed at Kubota Garden. He would then wait for the place to "speak" to him, as Jason Wirth describes in his essay (see page 111). He would imagine and construct gardens as a nurseryman, developing a unique contribution to the broader community of Issei gardeners and plantsmen that David Streatfield describes in his essay (see page 15). For garden design as practiced by Kubota was not merely the art of design—it was the capacity to listen, respect, and respond to the place as it is. He created the places and spaces for his gardens to emerge as distinct experiences that aggregate into a cohesive landscape.

As Kubota Garden was developed, it served both as a nursery for the plants needed by the gardening business and a garden, or rather a landscape of gardens. Kubota began by carving the land forms to allow a series of gardens to be placed throughout. He worked with local stone to establish the place for each garden, as described by Kentaro Kojima, drawing on the importance of stone in Japanese culture and the Shinto religion (see page 65). He then developed dozens of vignettes or small gardens that might inspire clients and visitors. It was a demonstration landscape and a living laboratory for Kubota and his community. As the business grew, Kubota developed a central road that allowed customers to drive through the gardens—what some have described as an automobile stroll garden or a drive-through nursery.[2] In this way he not only expanded the users of the landscape but offered a thoroughly modern means of moving through that landscape.

In 1941, despite the success of the nursery and design business, work stopped when the Kubota family was imprisoned by the American government (with the exception of his sons, Tom and Tak Kubota, who served in the U.S. Army). Incarcerated at Minidoka, Kubota took on the role of chief gardener creating, as Anna Tamura describes in her essay, a series of landscape and horticultural "camp beautification" projects during his three-year incarceration (see page 135). His gardens transformed the stripped and barren spaces "into places of respite, respect, and beauty." In 1945, the Kubota family was released and allowed to return home. While Fujitarō Kubota was able to regain use of his nursery, the garden had been left to its own devices: the roads taken over by weeds and the ponds silted up with debris. Jamie Ford's narrative (see page 151) describes this moment not as a garden lost, but a garden once loved, then neglected, and again loved. In returning, Kubota shifted the business to increase the land available for growing plants rather than for showing gardens, removing the flower gardens and other smaller gardens. He expanded the landscape to twenty-plus acres, giving him the space to cultivate rows upon rows of pine, arborvitae, yew, box, birch, cypress, spruce, and oak. Carefully pruned and trained specimen pines were a signature of the business and while many were sold to clients, many remain in the gardens.

In 1962, during the Century 21 World's Fair in Seattle, along the southern edge of the nursery, Kubota built the Mountainside, a landform rising sixty-five feet with ponds and waterfalls, a reference to both Mount Rainier, a local icon, and Mount Fuji, a Japanese icon. The mountain was constructed by importing 460 tons of rock and creating a series of waterfalls down the "mountain." Fed by a re-circulating pump and cistern system that draws water from the lower end of the series of ponds, the waterfalls appear natural, as if a spring were at the top of the mountain. Japanese ornaments including lanterns and arched bridges, a moon-viewing platform, and a moon bridge were added to the larger landscape.

After Kubota's death, there were development pressures; however, community leaders came together to preserve the important cultural landscape. They first successfully sought to landmark the Japanese American garden and then to assist the city in its acquisition of the property under a citywide open space program. In 1986 it was transferred to the care of Seattle Parks and Recreation and its head gardener, Don Brooks. Today these friends continue to sustain the landscape and its enduring story of immigration, resilience, and vision. And teachers such as Iain Robertson (see page 181) draw inspiration and use the garden to expand the imagination of students.

Fujitarō Kubota created a common land in Rainier Beach that equally, joyfully embraces the newly arrived, the long-residing, and the visiting. This collection of essays, images, and poems is a mosaic of distinct voices each reflecting on the experience of the landscape, the narratives it holds, and its significance over time to its many communities. It offers a means of exploring the garden, with its many entry points and circulation routes, each with its own narratives and poems waiting to be shared. It is a gift from those who have stewarded the garden alongside those artists and scholars who have come to deeply appreciate this outstanding place in our public realm. It comes to us at a time when we are each seeking ways to contribute to a more robust democracy and to return to a time when the immigrants were recognized for their leadership in forming this democracy we know as the United States of America.

Endnotes

1   Five of the top seven gardens are on the West Coast. See http://www.rothteien.com/ topics/na-survey.htm. Also see ibid., 9–26.

2   Robinson, Thomas M., "Traditions in Translation: The Gardens of Fujitaro Kubota" (Research, University of Washington, 1992).

3   Kubota tapped all the family's resources, including his children's savings, to make a down payment while a sympathetic friend lent his name to the transaction to get around the discriminatory ownership laws.

場所
place

The Nurserymen

David Streatfield

N 1972 THE Japanese government bestowed on Fujitarō Kubota the Fifth Order of the Sacred Treasure "for his achievements in his adopted country for introducing and building respect for Japanese gardening." This well-deserved accolade implicitly acknowledged Kubota's artistry, fine craftsmanship, business acumen, and his eminent place among Seattle Issei. But it blurs his unique artistic contribution to American garden design by suggesting that he was a figure who promoted an enthusiasm for traditional Japanese gardens. Thus, he was not celebrated for his unusual contribution to garden design of fusing traditional Japanese garden forms and native Pacific Northwestern plants. Furthermore, his social position among Seattle nurserymen is not acknowledged. Landscape and garden historians have largely ignored the work of nurserymen and concentrated on the roles played by landscape architects and other professional designers in shaping the garden tastes of the American upper and middle classes. American nurseries provided a critical alternative to the work of professional landscape architects that is a neglected history worthy of examination.

This essay provides a broad context for understanding Fujitarō Kubota's remarkable and unusual career as a confident, self-trained garden artist by examining how Seattle nurseries and nurserymen shaped middle- and upper-middle-class landscape tastes in public and private landscapes. It also examines how Issei gardeners and their nurseries served the much smaller needs of members of the local Japanese American community and fed the local upper-class fascination with aspects of *Japonisme.*

At the end of the nineteenth century, Frederick Law Olmsted, Sr. promoted a sweeping landscape vision introducing nature into the American city. This vision countered the ubiquitous American urban practice, established in the Colonial era, of allowing each property owner to create a house and garden expressing national origins, personal, or popular tastes. The Olmstedian landscape vision introduced nature into the city by establishing continuous masses of natural planting that included conserved natural areas and continuous parkways as well as broad tree-lined boulevards. This was complemented by the creation of planned subdivisions governed by carefully crafted design and social controls. These new landscapes were important foundations of the City Beautiful Movement.

These two forms of neighborhood landscape identity coexisted, presenting opposed images of uncontrolled, highly individualist expression and unified landscape control. Seattle nurseries served both landscape visions by supplying plants. Clients requiring design guidance were served by very few landscape architects on the West Coast. Consequently, civic leaders and upper-middle-class homeowners had little choice other than commissioning the leading national landscape architecture firm, The Olmsted Brothers. Founded in 1898 by John Charles Olmsted and Frederick Law Olmsted, Jr., the firm managed their numerous and extensive commissions from their office in Brookline, Massachusetts. This firm was responsible in the twentieth century for the design of new towns such as Palos Verdes, California; parks; park systems such as those of Seattle and Portland; university campuses; elite subdivisions such as The Highlands; large private estates; and gardens of varied size. Managing this panoply of widespread commissions involved frequent communication by telegraph and telephone, and lengthy train journeys.

FOR EACH OF THESE varied landscape commissions, this firm typically provided preliminary and final landscape designs, working drawings, and specifications, and supervised the design's execution. These services were relatively expensive; even some well-to-do Seattle private clients balked at the costs. It is, therefore, not at all surprising that professional landscape architects did not design smaller gardens in Seattle or larger domestic projects such as garden apartment projects. The paucity of landscape architecture offices and the high costs involved in employing landscape design firms such as The Olmsted Brothers led to some nurseries creating design departments

FACING Fujitarō Kubota trimming a pine at Seattle University, 1965.

to undertake the design and execution of a range of more modest and less prestigious design commissions. This was a critical alternative practice to employing landscape architects.

By 1910 eighteen nurseries and thirteen gardeners were listed in the Seattle street directories. By 1927 there were twenty-four nurseries and ten individuals listed as landscape architects and gardeners. Not all nurseries maintained design departments. Malmo Nursery was the leading Seattle nursery with a design division. Malmo boasted to their middle-class clients that their landscape department "enables you to secure the most effective and pleasing arrangements of the various details of garden architecture at the minimum cost." Malmo claimed to be able to provide the design and complete installation of the landscape of a private garden, and a wide range of garden structures, pergolas, fountains, rock gardens, stepping stone paths, and natural woodland gardens. In addition, they were able to provide designs for the landscape of public institutions, apartment houses, service stations, and factories, golf courses, and the planting arrangement of parking strips. The firm also proudly boasted of considerable success in "planting for immediate effect."[1]

Collectively, the design of parking strips, the front gardens of houses of modest size, and the entrance gardens of garden apartments by nursey design departments constitute a significant part of the street landscapes of several central residential neighborhoods. As far as is known, the designers at nurseries such as Malmo had a free hand in creating these public landscapes. Their heterogeneous nature contrasts strongly with the highly ordered street landscapes of the natural areas, public parks, and tree-lined boulevards designed by The Olmsted Brothers. But their abundance played a major role in shaping the city's emergent landscape identity. Indeed, the street landscapes created by the collective actions of nursery designers and private owners represent an emphatic statement of populist landscape taste.

The entrance courtyards of garden apartments are often an important presence on the city streets of central residential neighborhoods. These spaces functioned as highly visible entrance spaces to structures ranging in height from a single story to eight stories. They were designed to enhance the apartment building's architecture and social value within the local community. For example, the high visibility of the gardens of the Roy Vue Apartments on Capitol Hill and The Victoria Apartments on Queen Anne contributed significantly to their street landscapes, integrating the architecture of the apartment building into the fabric of the neighborhood.

INSET 1924 Malmo & Co. Planting Guide.

FACING Top row from left to right: Powell residence, 1968; residential project, 1926; Dunn Gardens, late 1920s. Middle row: residential project, late 1920s; residential project, late 1920s; Washington Federal Savings Bank, Bothell, 1963. Bottom row: Madison Park residence, late 1920s; Capitol Hill residence, 1926; May Kubota, residential project, 1926. Fujitarō Kubota hired professional photographers to take these to document his work.

1893~1924
NURSERY STOCK
SEEDS
PLANTING GUIDE
PRICE LIST
Spring
1924
MALMO & CO.
CORNER SIXTH AND STEWART AT WESTLAKE
SEATTLE, WASH.
THIRTY YEARS OF SATISFACTORY SERVICE.

Many street landscapes in Seattle's central neighborhoods were created by the design departments of nurseries and the uncoordinated actions of individual property owners. In marked contrast, most of the domestic gardens created by Issei nurserymen were *private* spaces seen only by their owners and friends. This may be a continuation of pervasive Japanese urban traditions. In Japan the grounds of temples, large villa gardens, and small gardens are invariably spaces that do not impinge visually on the landscape of the street. In Seattle the grounds of the private Jesuit Seattle University are the only work of an Issei nurseryman that is publically accessible.

Issei nurseries inevitably responded to differing sets of client commissions. Because the proprietors were prevented from attaining citizenship, the business of these nurseries was often limited to the sale of plants. Some nurseries also provided very basic garden maintenance services. But Issei nurserymen who attempted to provide more than the most basic maintenance tasks were invariably complete novices. Kamejiro Shioyama, who claimed to be the earliest Issei to begin a career as a gardener in about 1915, recalled that he learnt basic gardening techniques by working without pay at Bonnell's Nursery, at that time the largest nursery in Seattle and the provider of plants for many of The Olmsted Brothers' private gardens. He obtained instruction in more difficult professional gardening techniques by reading the *Manual of Gardening*. The Yamasaki and Nakamura nurseries were among the earliest nurseries to provide design services as well as sell plants. The formation of The Japanese Gardeners' Union in 1922 protected the interests of Issei nurseries.[2]

Fujitarō Kubota's experience as a garden designer and nurseryman was distinctly different from those of other Issei nurserymen. This reveals his remarkable and persistent determination to succeed in a profession for which he had no formal training. Born in 1880 as the eldest son of a rice farming family in Kōchi Prefecture on Shikoku Island, he was destined by custom to inherit the family farm. Despite his upbringing in a somewhat remote rural region of Japan, he evidently had other ambitions. After graduating from grammar school, he attended night classes at an agricultural training school where he learnt what he later described as "only a little introductory botany."[3] Nevertheless, he believed that this was more than most American gardeners knew; he derisively commented that "they didn't even know about the three ingredients of fertilizers and about which plants grow in the sun and which don't."[4]

It is not clear when Kubota decided that the making of gardens would become his controlling passion. He prepared for his chosen career as a garden designer by visiting and studying temple gardens to compensate for his lack of specific instruction in the art and techniques of garden making. He also visited Ritsurin Park, a former samurai estate in Takamatsu, a large city at the

FACING Kubota Garden nursery stock birch stand, 1975.

northern end of Shikoku Island. Begun by Takatoshi Ikoma, it was later taken over by the samurai Matsudaira family who owned it until the Meiji Restoration. Like many aristocratic gardens, it then became a public park. Consequently, Kubota was among the first generation of young Japanese men who profited by having access to formerly inaccessible private estates.

Ritsurin Park is a notable example of a stroll garden. It clearly influenced Kubota's approach to garden design. The spatial structure of this unusually large garden is defined by a series of large mounds and a chain of six ponds. The range of planting is unusual since it contains a wide variety of species and plant arrangements. Palm trees, bamboos, pines, and deciduous trees co-exist with pampas and other grasses arranged in unusual combinations.

An equally formative experience for Kubota may have been traversing the hills and gorges south of Takamatsu, which are remarkably similar to the foothills of the Cascade Range in Washington state. The experience of travelling through these gorges may well have inspired his most distinctive use of rocks.

Kubota arrived in San Francisco in 1907 and worked in a sawmill. He worked his way up the coast and eventually arrived in Seattle. During the First World War his family managed a hotel and an apartment house, which were sold at the end of the war. He opened his nursery in 1923. He was evidently keenly aware of the shortcomings of his education, which was limited to his very basic education and the botany class. He returned to Japan three times seeking instruction in the techniques of garden making. As he recalled, this "was not easy... [I]n Kyoto I visited professional gardeners and asked many questions, but they wouldn't give me most part of their know-how."[5] Kubota evidently felt that the highly refined arts of poetry, the tea ceremony, ikebana, and traditional dancing were taught in a socially rigid manner unavailable to those born outside the system. Lacking access to the traditional instruction in these aristocratic arts, he acknowledged his friend Ryotaro Nishikawa, who came from Okayama Prefecture, as his sole teacher. Nishikawa had learned design techniques from his father. The son was particularly adept at cultivating pine trees and helped Kubota whenever he had time. When Kubota felt that he was having difficulties with his garden designs, he went "into the woods and prayed to the gods for help."[6]

KUBOTA'S DESIGN APPROACH is demonstrated clearly at what is now known as Kubota Garden. Starting in 1929, he slowly amassed an area of over twenty acres. Kubota Garden functioned as a display garden demonstrating the range of design features that his nursery could provide. In addition, it functioned as the location of the Kubota family home and a center for hosting Issei and other community events.

FACING Lower Garden with family and Kubota Gardening Company crew, 1930.

Kubota did not try to create an "authentic" Japanese garden. No drawings were made. By using plants that flourished in this climate and accommodating American cultural traditions, Kubota merged traditional Japanese design forms with the needs of contemporary American living patterns. Potential clients could view different techniques for building retaining walls, the use of modernist paving designs, and the important play of light on plants. As Thomas Robinson pointed out, the installation of a circular drive through the central part of the garden enabled well-to-do clients to drive through the garden. This was clearly not a traditional Japanese garden. This probably explains why Juki Iida did not engage Kubota in the construction of the Japanese Garden in the Washington Park Arboretum despite Kubota's prominence as the best-known Issei nurseryman in Seattle.

The merging of some American modernist forms and plants suitable for the Pacific Northwest with traditional Japanese ideas distinguishes Kubota's gardens from those of other Issei in Seattle. Most earlier "Japanese" gardens in the eastern states were created by Issei in traditional Japanese styles. Kubota's approach to garden design as a form of placemaking acknowledged and celebrated the character of the Pacific Northwest region.

Kubota's design approach lent itself particularly well to the creation of small gardens. Terry Welch has kindly provided the bill Kubota produced for designing and constructing his uncle's small garden near Seward Park in the late 1950s. Kubota specified 150 tons of high Cascade granite, one hundred cubic yards of topsoil, thirty yards of crushed gravel, together with "All labor and machinery required and all the Plant material." The bill concluded with the memorable statement emphasizing Kubota's supreme self-confident artistic vision that "Mr Kubota will plant the garden as he sees fit."[7]

The design departments of Seattle nurseries played a considerable but unacknowledged role in fashioning the character of its residential neighborhoods. The character of most of Seattle's residential streets has been fashioned by the design of the garden spaces of private gardens and apartment buildings. Nurseries provided the plants and also promoted and provided design ideas about urban form and design. Collectively, the emergent heterogeneous street landscape stands in contrast to the unified vision of continuous nature promoted by landscape architects and City Beautiful advocates. The lack of recognition of the critical contribution made by the design division of nurseries may in part be attributed to an American lack of respect for labor's contributions to national identity and a distinct distaste for the hand labor involved in what is now defined as design-build practice.

In contrast, Issei nurseries in Seattle provided plants and, in some cases, basic maintenance services that were far less visible since their number was considerably smaller. There were of course

FACING Detail from Kubota's landscape design at Seattle University, 1965.

front gardens that displayed an affinity for Japanese ideas. But generally, the gardens fashioned by Issei nurseries were far less visible, extending the Japanese tradition of gardens providing critical opportunities for the contemplation of nature in more private settings. In Seattle only the campus of Seattle University made such spaces generally available.

It is therefore ironic that Fujitarō Kubota became the best-known nurseryman in this region. Kubota's important contribution of melding Japanese forms and concepts with Pacific Northwest plants and living patterns is unique. An astute businessman, he recognized the necessity for adjusting the forms of traditional Japanese garden models by using native plants of the Pacific Northwest region and accommodating new programmatic necessities. It was this that enabled him to transcend his humble roots and lack of formal training in the art of garden design. That this artistic achievement has been recognized both in Japan and in the Pacific Northwest region is surely a most welcome development of cultural reconciliation.

FACING Fujitarō Kubota at work; son-in-law George Yano stands in the truck, 1950.

Endnotes

1   Malmo Nursery catalog, 1928.

2   Ito, Kazuo, *Issei: A History of Japanese Immigrants in North America* (Seattle: Executive Committee of Japanese Community Service, 1973).

3   Ibid.

4   Ibid.

5   Ibid.

6   Ibid

7   Welch, Terry (letter to author, 2018).

場所

ashide no yo*
(Garden Poem)

an Eastern red-eared terrapin
turtle moves with the pace of stone

the long crawl out Lake Washington
into the daylight of Mapes Creek

site of an old stump farm
evoking land clear cut and harvested

in the time of the Heian period;
to imagine a woodland forest

where one was once *removed*

transformed by rock, stood
upright to impart the heart-

spirit, horsetail rushes embedded
in a boulder, forty million years ago

permutations of the natural order,
flow through weeping spruce

there in the cataract of blue atlas,
water slapping against stone

an orange koi glides
alongside a choir of black carp,

the bronze bell still throbbing

* The Reed Style of gardening that mimicked a painting style which concealed short messages, or were overwritten with poems.

SHIN YU PAI

The Garden(s) of Arrival

Jeffrey Hou

LOCATED IN SOUTH SEATTLE, the twenty-acre Kubota Garden is one of the finest gardens built by the early Japanese immigrants as they settled into their new home on the other side of the Pacific. The garden's story represents a family's struggle, achievement, and perseverance through hard times. This story is one that many immigrants have shared though not always in the same way. While not everyone was as accomplished as Fujitarō Kubota in creating such a magnificent work of art, gardening either as a humble act of recreation, an expression of one's culture and identity, or as a means of making a living is an activity that many people, immigrants or not, have experienced.

For immigrants or those who have moved to a new place from far away, gardening carries perhaps even more significance as a both bodily and symbolic act of putting down roots. This short essay explores the commonality between Kubota Garden and acts of gardening in many immigrant communities. Specifically, it examines the range of ways that people find meaning, form connections, and support themselves through the garden and the act of gardening. Gardens, as such, signify one's arrival at a place, through acts of laboring, learning, negotiating, and adapting.

FACING The garden's Entry Gate was designed by Gerard Tsutakawa.

In Seattle's International District, where Kubota family once lived, gardening now finds new expressions in the 1.5-acre Danny Woo International District Community Garden, a place created during the community activism of the 1970s when the neighborhood was threatened by the construction of the Kingdome. During the protest movement against the project, the garden served as an act of positive transformation, a space of hope for the community. Today, the Kingdome no longer exists, but the garden continues to thrive and serve as an important personal and social space for nearly a hundred gardeners, most of them recent immigrants.

It was here in the Danny Woo Garden where I began to learn firsthand about the social significance of gardening, and where my ongoing research on community gardening started. In learning about the history of Kubota Garden, I find it remarkable how the story of a garden built nearly a century ago echoes that of immigrant gardening today. The linkages, I believe, tell us something important about the significance of Kubota Garden and what it embodies in the North American cultural landscapes.

A Place of Survival and Livelihood

In a study on community gardens in Seattle that my colleagues, former students, and I conducted over a decade ago,[1] we found that gardening, particularly in gardens with predominantly immigrant gardeners, was not only a recreational activity like those in middle-class neighborhoods. It was also a means of supporting oneself economically. For immigrants and refugees with limited language and job skills, and particularly those from an agrarian background, gardening is a way to supplement one's income and reduce family expenses. It allows one to apply skills and knowledge. At Thistle P-Patch in southeast Seattle, the priority on crop production for the predominantly Mien gardeners is reflected in the arrangement of the plots that leaves very little space for anything else on the site. The intensive use of the garden signifies the purpose of the garden, distinct from its counterparts in the more affluent neighborhoods in Seattle.

While Kubota Garden was not used for food production, it functioned in much the same way as a place that once supported the Kubota family's gardening and nursery business, a function that was shared by many Issei gardens built around the time.[2] More than a place for personal leisure and enjoyment, it was used as a demonstration garden to show customers the plants they would purchase and also the kind of garden that the Kubotas could create. "Customers could drive in and see the water features, trees, and stones."[3] Like Kubota Garden, gardens of the Harui, Nishitani, and Seike families in Seattle were also built on the grounds of nurseries, businesses, and homes.[4] With racial discrimination and bias in the early days of Japanese immigration,

agriculture and gardening provided a means of economic survival for immigrants, many of whom were skilled farmers. Without formal training in gardening, many of them were self-taught, using their agricultural knowledge and skills, including Fujitarō Kubota.

As the Japanese returned from the prison camps after World War II, the gardening business became especially important. Faced with economic hardship and continued racial prejudice, gardening was one of the only viable means of livelihood. "Those with agricultural skills could convert that to the gardening business."[5] In the case of the Kubotas, the garden enabled them to return home to Seattle after the war. They went on to rebuild their business and become involved in creating many significant landmarks in the Pacific Northwest, including the Seattle Center, the Japanese Garden at the Bloedel estate (now the Bloedel Reserve) on Bainbridge Island, and the plantings on the Seattle University campus.

A Place of Social Gathering and Community Building

Contrary to the perception of private, personal enjoyment, gardens can be an important place of social gathering and community building. In fact, many studies of community gardens have shown community building to rank prominently among their many benefits. In a 2012 survey conducted for the American Community Gardening Association, 66% of the respondents identified social engagement, community building, or neighborhood revitalization as one of the most significant benefits of community gardens, second only to food production and access.[6] Another study that reviews the available research on community gardens found "social development/cohesion" to be the top motivation, followed by consumption of fresh food and health improvement.[7] The social function of gardening can be particularly important for immigrant gardeners. In a study that documents the use of gardens by Hmong refugees, Giraud notes, "Having a garden offers a social outlet, as well as a place to use daily skills from their homeland."[8] In a case study of community gardens in Oakland, California, Prince finds the garden to function as an everyday place for intercultural learning and interactions among residents of different cultural and ethnic backgrounds.

One of my early encounters with the immigrant gardeners at the Danny Woo Garden was through a PhotoVoice survey conducted to find out about the design preferences of the gardeners for a green street. We gave each participating gardener a disposable camera to take pictures of what they liked and disliked in the garden and the surrounding neighborhood. As expected, most gardeners took pictures of plants and structures in the garden and sometimes landmarks in the neighborhood, except for one elderly gardener, Mr. Su, who came back with pictures of all the friends he met in the garden. He said, "making friends was the most important part of gardening." As a newly arrived immigrant and resident in the neighborhood, he knew very few people until he started to garden at the Danny Woo Garden. He went on to mention that talking to friends was especially important to elderly people.[9]

Issei gardens were important social spaces for the Japanese community especially during the period of racial discrimination when it was hard for the Japanese to find places for community events and social functions. Kubota Garden has served as a center for social and cultural activities for the Japanese community in Seattle.[10] Similarly, the Mukai Garden on Vashon Island has also been a place for weddings, Buddhist ceremonies, and cherry blossom parties.[11] At Kubota Garden, it has been mentioned that although it was not a public garden, Fujitarō Kubota would allow access to the garden to almost anyone. It has been used for field trips by schoolchildren in the neighborhood, and "a manicured picnic lawn was kept for the neighbors to use for picnics."[12] The generosity of the Kubotas was likely one of the reasons that they were able to return successfully to the community in southeast Seattle, and also the reason that the neighbors came together to protect the property from being sold to developers in the 1980s.

A Place of Adaptation and Resilience

In their seminal 1990 volume, *The Meaning of Gardens*, Mark Francis and Randolph T. Hester, Jr., explore gardens as idea, place, and action. They argue that the garden is a place to meditate, reflect, and escape from conflict, and that "One cannot fully examine the garden as a physical place without probing the ideas that generated the selection of its materials and the making of its geometry."[13] For immigrant and ethnic gardeners, the garden is also a site for contemplating and reconstructing their sense of place in an unfamiliar environment. At the South Central Farm in Los Angeles, before its demolition after a three-year struggle, the fourteen-acre site served as a place for communities of Mesoamerican descent to practice farming and self-reliance to foster a strong sense of place.[14] Although the place no longer exists, the gardeners have continued to farm at an alternative site. In a 2004 study of community gardens in New York City, Saldivar-Tanaka and Krasny found that the gardens provide a connection between immigrants and their cultural heritage. The Latino gardens seemed to be particularly important as sites for maintaining Puerto Rican farming culture in an urban environment.[15]

At Kubota Garden, creating a sense of place was also critical to understanding its significance, one that embodies a process of adaptation and finding one's place between homes and cultures. On the one hand, the garden represents the culture of Japan, as Fujitarō had hoped the garden

especially when shared with friends, family, and loved ones. But beyond its visual and experiential characteristics, the garden also embodies a story of struggle shared by many immigrants and their families. Their gardens, like the one built by the Kubotas, are places of both labor and comfort, places of perseverance and hope. It is through these engagements that the gardens become places of arrival in a once foreign and unfamiliar land. Seattle is fortunate to have acquired Kubota Garden as a city park in the 1980s. What was once one family's hard work and struggle is now a place many can visit and experience. As a site that holds memories, Kubota Garden is a place of healing and learning. As a place of ongoing engagement and transformation, it is a place of continued discovery and renewal. As such, the garden signifies our collective future.

Endnotes

1   Hou, J., Johnson, J.M., Lawson, L.J. (2009) *Greening Cities, Growing Communities: Learning from Seattle's Urban Community Gardens.* Seattle: University of Washington Press.

2   Tochihara, T.K. (2003) *A Generation of Gardens: Japanese Style Gardens of the Issei in Seattle.* Master of Arts thesis, Cornell University.

3   Kubota Garden Foundation. (2017) *Kubota Garden Tour Guide Manual.* Seattle: Kubota Garden Foundation.

4   Tochihara.

5   Tochihara, 102.

6   Lawson, L., Drake, L. (2013) Community gardening organization survey 2011-2012. *Community Greening Review* 18: 20–47.

7   Guitart, D., Pickering, C., Byrne, J. (2012) Past results and future directions in urban community gardens research. *Urban Forestry and Urban Greening* 11(4): 364–373.

8   Giraud, D.D. (1990) Shared Backyard Gardening. In Francis, M., Hester, Jr. R. (eds.), *The Meaning of Gardens.* Cambridge, MA: The MIT Press.

9   Hou, J. (2013) Transcultural Participation: Designing with Immigrant Communities in Seattle's International District. In Hou, J. (ed.), *Transcultual Cities: Border Crossing and Placemaking,* 222–236. London and New York: Routledge.

10   Tochihara.

11   Tochihara, David Streatfield cited, n.d.

12   Parmeter, M.A. (2010) A Short History of the Kubota Garden in Rainier Beach, Seattle, Washington. Unpublished manuscript.

13   Francis, M., Hester, Jr. R. (eds.) (1990) *The Meaning of Gardens.* Cambridge, MA: The MIT Press. 8.

14   Mare, T.M., Peña, D.G. (2010) Urban agriculture in the making of insurgent spaces in Los Angeles and Seattle. In Hou, J. (ed.), *Insurgent Public Space: Guerrilla Urbanism and the Remaking of Contemporary Cities,* 241–254. London and New York: Routledge.

15   Saldivar-Tanaka, L., Krasny, M.E. (2004) Culturing community development, neighborhood open space, and civic agriculture: the case of Latino community gardens in New York City. *Agriculture and Human Values* 21: 399–412.

16   Tochihara. Interview with Tom Kubota, 32.

17   Tochihara, 98.

18   Ibid, 99.

would "promote goodwill and give Americans a better appreciation of the culture of Japan."[16] On the other hand, Fujitarō blended traditional garden elements with materials that he could find locally. As a result, the garden became more a work of adaptation and his own artistic sensibility. "Fujitarō Kubota's philosophy was to work with nature... [He] sensed what was appropriate and accordingly placed rocks, trees, nursery materials, or a good Japanese plant."[17] According to Earl Layman,the development of the garden was never intended to produce an authentic Japanese garden. "Rather, it was conceived to serve as a demonstrative exhibit for clients, and to provide the community with a garden to be proud of." [18]

The process of adaptation is one of the reasons a garden can become resilient. Today, much like the way Fujitarō Kubota acquired more and more land to expand the garden and just as the Kubotas kept adding new elements to the site, the garden continues to be a work in progress with new features being added and work that involves participation of supporters and volunteers. Specifically, a strolling garden was added in 1999 with help of volunteers. Other additions include an entry gate designed by sculptor Gerard Tsutakawa, the Terrace Overlook, and a new area called the Maple Woods. There were also regular work parties with forest stewards and other volunteers to remove invasive species and to plant native ones. These new elements and continued efforts make Kubota Garden a living and resilient garden, as envisioned by Fujitarō Kubota.

An Extraordinary Garden with a Shared Narrative

In retelling aspects of Kubota Garden's story alongside those of other immigrant gardens, my intent is to underscore the common narrative shared by immigrant experiences across space and time. The story of Kubota Garden that began nearly a century ago echoed those of recent immigrants in North America and beyond. For the Kubotas and other immigrants, the garden is *a place of survival and livelihood, a place of social gathering and community building,* and *a place of adaptation and resilience.* By drawing these parallels between the common narratives of these immigrant gardens and gardeners, we can begin to see the greater significance of Kubota Garden, particularly in this time and age. Today, as many nations and societies struggle with political divisiveness and longstanding social and cultural biases, the stories of Kubota Garden and many other gardens are an important source of lessons and inspiration. They remind us what has happened before, how far we have come, what barriers continue to exist, and what can bring community and society together.

With the hard work of supporters and volunteers, Kubota Garden today is a place of extraordinary beauty. A stroll in the garden presents a timeless experience, a collective enjoyment

THE UNITED STATES OF AMERICA

ORIGINAL
TO BE GIVEN TO
THE PERSON NATURALIZED

CERTIFICATE OF NATURALIZATION

No. 7271516

Petition No. 48770

Personal description of holder as of date of naturalization: Date of birth February 27, 1880 ; *sex* Male ;
complexion Sallow *color of eyes* Brown ; *color of hair* Gray ; *height* 5 *feet* 1 *inches:*
weight 130 *pounds; visible distinctive marks* Scar on left side of mouth
Marital status Widowed *former nationality* Japanese
I certify that the description above given is true, and that the photograph affixed hereto is a likeness of me.

sign here →

Fujitaro Kubota
(Complete and true signature of holder)

United States of America
} ss:
Western District of Washington

Be it known, that at a term of the U. S. District *Court of*
Western District of Washington, Northern Division,
held pursuant to law at Seattle, Washington
on November 21, 1955 *the Court having found that*
FUJITARO KUBOTA
then residing at 9817 - 55th Ave. South, Seattle, Washington
intends to reside permanently in the United States (when so required by the Naturalization Laws of the United States), had in all other respects complied with the applicable provisions of such naturalization laws, and was entitled to be admitted to citizenship, thereupon ordered that such person be and (s)he was admitted as a citizen of the United States of America.
In testimony whereof the seal of the court is hereunto affixed this 21st
day of November *in the year of our Lord nineteen hundred and*
fifty-five *and of our Independence, the one hundred*
and eightieth.

Seal

MILLARD P. THOMAS
Clerk of the UNITED STATES DISTRICT *Court.*
By E. M. Groff *Deputy Clerk.*

It is a violation of the U.S. Code (and punishable as such) to copy, print, photograph, or otherwise illegally use this certificate.

DEPARTMENT OF JUSTICE

The Neighborhood Responds

Alex Gallo-Brown

ON THE KIND OF dismal morning in late November that encourages lying around in one's sweatpants with a mug of green tea, I instead zipped my hooded jacket to my chin and made the short drive from south Beacon Hill, where I live, to Rainier Beach, the southeasternmost neighborhood of Seattle where Kubota Garden, the once private and now public testimonial to the life and work of master gardener Fujitarō Kubota, has stood for more than ninety years. I arrived to an uncharacteristically empty garden—no cars thronging the parking lot and no people hiking the forested paths. Drawing my hood over my head, I sidestepped the fast-collecting pools of rainwater, admiring constructed ponds and waterfalls as I reflected on moments of private pain and memories of personal joy.

This is one way to use Kubota Garden—as a refuge, a site for meditation and healing. Marcus Harrison Green, a longtime resident of Rainier Beach and former reporter of *The Seattle Times,* recited lyrics from the Persian poet Rumi when I asked him to describe his relationship to the garden: "Come, come, whoever you are. Wanderer, worshipper, come, come, even if you've broken your vows a thousand times, come again. This is not a caravan of despair. This love is here for you." Green, who is black, was born and raised in lower-income, majority-minority Rainier Beach but attended a mostly white, private high school in Burien. Beset by pressures from both sides, he came to Kubota Garden during high school to find temporary peace. "I was straddling two worlds," he explains. "[I was going to] this private, extremely affluent, extremely white school in Burien and then coming back to [Rainier] Beach, which was kind of the hood at that time, just trying to survive. I didn't really fit in anywhere. Kubota Garden was where I fit in."

Race is not incidental to the story of Kubota Garden. Indeed, it is central. Founded as a horticultural laboratory and display center for Japanese immigrant Fujitarō Kubota's gardening business in 1927, the garden became dormant in 1942 after Fujitarō and his family were forcibly removed from their homes and transported to the Minidoka Relocation Center in south central Idaho. (Improbably, Fujitarō, ever the community-minded green thumb, managed to construct a public garden *inside his own concentration camp.*) Upon returning to Seattle in 1945, the Kubotas revived their garden and restarted their business, mounting notable installations on the grounds of Seattle University and the Bloedel Reserve on Bainbridge Island as well as in numerous private homes throughout the region. At the same time, the Rainer Beach Kubota Garden became a hub of Japanese American social and cultural activity, functioning as a quasi-public, quasi-private space for the Japanese community for decades.

As the Kubotas rose in stature, the neighborhood around their garden began to change. Ron Angeles, a long-time community liaison for the City of Seattle's Department of Neighborhoods, remembers playing baseball against Rainer Beach High School in the 1960s while a student at Chief Sealth High School in West Seattle. Back then, most of the Beach players were white and Asian, says Angeles, who is Filipino American. By 1979, when he began serving the Rainier Valley as a community liaison, the neighborhood "was pretty much split in thirds—a third Asian, a third black, a third white. The black population was increasing because black folks were coming down from the Central Area, and there was bussing [so] white folks were pretty much taking off [for the suburbs]. And then we started [housing] immigrants and refugees." Today, the neighborhood is 31% African American, 31% Asian, 13% Hispanic, and 14% mixed race, according to the advocacy group Rainier Beach Action Coalition. Only about a quarter of residents identify as white. More than half speak multiple languages.

The diversity of Rainier Valley generally, and of Rainier Beach in particular, is all the more astonishing given the almost total whiteness that one finds in much of the rest of the city. Sizable populations of Vietnamese, Somalis, and Filipinos reside alongside communities of African-Americans and Latinos. Recently arrived immigrants from Africa and Asia live next door to second- and third-generation immigrants from Africa and Asia. Mosques hold services blocks away from Jewish synagogues and Catholic churches.

FACING *(clockwise from top left)*: Soapstone carving event; Roxanne Sklar and Lisa Kajimura play the koto at 1990 annual meeting; performance by the Rainbow Chorus conducted by Thomas Minami at 1996 annual meeting; Fujitarō Kubota's great-grandchildren, Chrissie *(left, in kimono)* and Tara, at 1990 annual meeting.

The area's diversity is not the result of happenstance, of course. Despite Seattle's reputation as a progressive bastion, the city's history is as tarnished with racism, red-lining, and social exclusion as any other. People of color historically gathered in south Seattle because they were prohibited or discouraged from living anywhere else. In this sense, Seattle is merely typical. What makes southeast Seattle exceptional, says Nora Liu, longtime anti-racist advocate and co-author of the City of Seattle's Equitable Development Initiative, is the relative harmony and lack of fixed boundaries that exist among racial, cultural, and ethnic groups. "In a lot of other cities, the Irish are here, the African Americans are here, the Puerto Ricans are here, and so on," says Liu, pointing to an imaginary map. "Here, though, there is all of this mixing." Liu references the noted sociologist Sherryl Cashin, who repeatedly cited Rainier Valley as an example of the difference between *desegregation* (the ending of social exclusion for previously disenfranchised groups) and *integration* (the conscious inclusion and empowerment of historically marginalized people) in her book *The Failures of Integration: How Race and Class Are Undermining the American Dream*.

Kubota Garden is part of Rainier Valley's history of racial integration and co-habitation. In the early 1980s, after Rainier Beach was targeted by condominium developers, the garden was designated a historical landmark by the city of Seattle. Six years later, the Kubotas sold their property to the city, which has maintained the garden as a public park ever since. Antonia Angeles Hare, a lifelong resident of Rainier Beach, remembers visiting the garden as a child with her friends and telling ghost stories at night after the park had closed. Now a new mother, she routinely brings her children to the park to "forest bathe." By exposing them to the air and pollens of the garden, she hopes to strengthen their immune systems. The garden is a vital resource for the community, she says, in part because it serves as a welcoming space for people of color. "You go there to escape a lot of different things," says Hare, who is Filipina and white. "The fact that it has grown to be a place that everybody in the community can enjoy but it's not a white pillar [is important]. It's a minority space that everybody can enjoy for its beauty."

The sense of communal togetherness that Kubota Garden inspires is at least as important as the solace that it confers to individuals, community members say. "I love the park because there are people from so many backgrounds there," says Liu. "There are kids hanging out, elders going for walks, ranges in age, race, and ethnicity. Kubota Garden allows for people to bump into each other informally. If you and I are walking in Kubota, maybe we don't stop and have a talk but we just wave at each other, and it starts bridging that network and community." Green echoes Liu's emphasis of the necessity of communal public space in a rapidly gentrifying city. Kubota Garden "is a necessary contrast to all this shift and displacement and aggressive alteration and

FACING This local costume designer dons her latest creation to see how it feels on a stroll through the garden.

transformation of the city's character [that are happening now]," he says. "Places that provoke community and togetherness [are] very important." Angeles agrees, stressing the sense of pride and ownership that community members feel for a garden that they view as belonging to them. "It's our place," Angeles says, thumping the table. "That's ours. I've heard that people will go expecting a traditional Japanese garden, but Kubota's different. Kubota's the blending of the natural Pacific Northwest environment with the Japanese feel, with lanterns, ponds, and plants cut in a different way. But you still see the pine trees. It's also an American garden."

Hare, Liu, Green, and Angeles movingly describe the role that the garden has played in their communities for decades. But the neighborhood is once again changing. In 2017, the average home value in the city of Seattle surpassed $800,000, making it one of the most expensive urban spaces in the country to own a home. As a result, the city's middle classes, in search of cheaper housing, have begun to move south, displacing previous community members and whitening spaces formerly occupied by people of color. These economic and demographic shifts pose serious questions for the future of Kubota Garden. Will the garden be valued as highly by residents who can afford to purchase their recreation privately? Will the addition of more affluent and more white faces threaten the garden's reputation as a haven for people of color? Who is Kubota Garden for?

Viewed in this context, my recent sojourn to an empty garden acquires a different resonance altogether. I imagine a future Rainier Beach where the diversity has ebbed as surely as it once flowed, new and more-affluent residents, perhaps in possession of their own private gardens, no longer place the same value on public space, and cross-cultural exchange is unnecessary because almost everyone looks the same. This is a dystopian and frankly depressing vision, and one that need not come to pass. The crisis of unaffordable housing and the accompanying neighborhood gentrification and community displacement are the results of decades of local policymaking that prioritized capital over community and private property over public space. These are decisions—political and social choices—that may yet be reversed.

In the meantime, amidst all that change, astride all that loss, Kubota Garden continues to stand as a testimonial not only to the achievements of Fujitarō Kubota and the gardeners who have come after him but also to the very concept of public space—land owned by the public to be used for the benefit of all. Kubota Garden will endure. Whether or not it continues to serve as a gathering place for the myriad community and cultures who surround it is an open question, one that will be decided by policymakers, residents, and advocacy groups in the years to come.

Says Liu: "Part of the reason that Kubota is special is because of the community it serves. The question now becomes can it be used as an anchor to hold people in place?"

精神

spirit

The Importance of Stone

Kentaro Kojima

WHEN I INTERVIEWED several architects and landscapers for this essay, I asked their opinion about the most profound influence that Japanese gardens have brought to the Pacific Northwest. The answer was unanimous: the use of stone. This is in part because of the work of Fujitarō Kubota.

No two stones are identical. Every stone is unique and has its own presence and energy. Japanese gardens use this uniqueness to its fullest.

Japanese gardens are motivated and inspired by the natural landscape. The awe one feels when looking at a natural landscape and the sensation that we are in the presence of something magnificent is what moves Japanese gardeners to create their gardens. These gardeners do not try to replicate nature. Instead, they seek to draw out the essence of what is impressive about a natural scene and use it in their design.

Of the design elements a designer of a Japanese garden has to work with, stone is arguably the most important, or at least the most elemental. Stone is often regarded as the bone structure on which everything else in the garden is built. For this reason, the importance of stone in a Japanese garden cannot be overstated. Stone has an almost reverential status in these gardens, and the greatest of care is taken in its selection and placement. Japanese gardens are fundamentally different from other traditional gardens in that they are designed to be spaces for contemplation, spirituality (without any specific religious connotation), and healing. While stone is perhaps the most important element in a Japanese garden, it is still used with other elements to achieve these ultimate goals.

The gardener first decides on the stone arrangement, giving the garden its bone structure, then adds plants, making the plants subservient or complementary to the stone. All elements are employed toward the ultimate end of creating a beautiful scene.

Water is also central to the Japanese garden. Even when water is impossible to access, Japanese sensibility still calls for water to be represented in some form. This is why dry-waterscapes, *kare-sansui* (dry landscapes), *kare-taki* (dry waterfalls), and other metaphorical waterscapes came into being.

Some famous temple gardens used these design ideas to great results. Historically, Japanese gardens have tried to represent nature, but some took the symbolism much further, creating gardens that became purely abstract.

The most famous of these gardens is the one in Ryoan-ji created in the late fifteenth century. The abstract nature of the design resists easy interpretation. There are many theories as to what was the intention and what the stone arrangement means. One interpretation posits that the garden is a stone koan, a paradox to be meditated upon.

Whatever the truth, there is no doubt these stones used in the gardens are intriguing. Stones are intrinsically intriguing, even if you are not a scholar of Japanese gardens. Children often play and collect stones. We name stones when we go hiking. There seems to be something visceral about stone that speaks to us. It is these visceral, emotion-evoking characteristics of stone that the Japanese gardeners work with.

The near veneration of stone in Japanese gardens seems to be, in part, rooted in the human perception of stones as being invincible. This could be said about water as well.

Stone and water give, but they also take away. They are different from plants, which grow and change with us. Plants keep on giving and rarely, if ever, take.

We can't beat water or stone, so we respect and fear them. But we want them around, maybe because they seem distant and indifferent to us. Stone and water, thus, are closer to *kami* (god/spirit) than other objects. This also might be part of the reason Japanese gardeners insist on using "untouched" (unfabricated) stone.

Experienced Japanese gardeners and masons often say that the stone "tells" them where it wants to be placed and which way it wants to face. This sounds very esoteric, but when you start

paying attention to the intrigue that stirs in you when you see a stone or a group of them, you start to understand what the more experienced people are saying when they tell you to listen to the "voice of the stone."

THERE ARE MANY TERMS AND TECHNIQUES in the canons of stone arrangement. They can sound quite esoteric. But as you pay attention to your intuitive response to stones in nature and in gardens and study good examples of stone arrangement, you will find it difficult to avoid using seemingly contradictory terms such as "movement" or "energy" and "flow" to describe the stones.

For example, let's say you were to work with a stone that has a tapered top and a middle that flares out like a skirt, ending with a bowl shape towards the bottom. If you bury the stone, with the tapered top above ground past the point where it starts to round in, it will look stable. But if you expose the undercut, then all of a sudden the stone looks unstable and a lot smaller.

Maybe the tapered top has a lean to it. That lean makes the stone look like it is heading in that direction (this is the "energy" or "flow" of the stone). You can use this movement to direct the observer's eyes.

FACING Terrace Overlook, Kubota Garden. Artist Gerard Tsutakawa designed the railing. Seattle Parks and Recreation carpenters built the wood structure.

INSET The *ishigaki* (dry stone) wall was built in 2014 during a workshop led by Junji and Suminori Awata, fourteenth- and fifteenth-generation stone masons from Japan.

Stone demands a response. Reading this, you may not understand what I am getting at, but when you actually put stone on the ground, you will inevitably have a response. The stone dictates the quality of the space and forces a response from you, maybe even an unconscious one. Quieting your mind and observing your response helps you to create a nonverbal word. As you build your language word by word over time, then and only then can you attempt to create poetry with stone. This is the reason many master gardeners and master masons insist on having their apprentices learn the spirit/heart (*kokoro*) of the art and not just the technique. It is your spirit, after all, that will create the art; the technique is there as a means to let you do that.

If this all sounds mystical and distantly spiritual, I would argue that when you start paying attention to your surroundings and consciously noting your responses, you will also end up adopting these sorts of expressions.

If you are still unconvinced that humans have a visceral response to stone, consider what you feel when you climb into the mountains and see large, sharp, rugged rocks. (The difference between "rock" and "stone" is that rock is in situ and stone is removed from its original place. In Japanese, rock is spelled 岩 and stone 石, the difference being that trident-shaped thing (山) on top, which means mountain. So, stones still in the mountains are rocks.) Those standing rocks in the mountains are powerful, strong, and wild—intimidating, even. They are exposed to harsh weather and embody rough and sudden movements.

Compare that with rocks you see in lower altitudes that are flatter and smoother (like a "lying cow," as we say in Japanese). These rocks are calmer and friendlier, more approachable and more stable than their rugged counterparts above. Noticing these basic differences is one way for you to start to "hear" what the stone is telling you.

Another simple experiment you can do is to find the primary view (the "face") of the stone and bury it halfway. (The primary view simply means the side of the stone that appeals to you.) Then, dig up the stone, roll it, and re-bury it. You will have a markedly different experience every time you roll the stone and bury it halfway.

While there is a lot of terminology to remember and a lot of do's and don'ts, over time, you will begin to appreciate how stones make you feel. Does the stone seem like it is out of balance? Like it is not rooted in the ground? Does it feel like it grows in size when you bury it in a certain way? Does it lean? Does it sit still or is it suggesting movement?

Ultimately, you have to come to a place where you are comfortable. And that's the start of stone arrangement.

As in any creative endeavor, the rules will be useful as a springboard in the beginning, but should not limit one's sensibility and creativity. At some point, you will find yourself casting some of the taboos aside and experimenting, as you should, because stones have almost infinite potential to display personality and character. It is up to the garden designer to harness that potential.

FUJITARŌ KUBOTA, while not formally trained in traditional Japanese gardening, had a great sensibility for stone and other elements. One could argue that because of his lack of formal training in Japanese gardens, he was able to be more experimental and flexible. This trait surely worked well when he had to come up with garden designs that pleased his clients.

The natural scenery in the Pacific Northwest is remarkably similar to that of Japan. Both are mountainous, have a lot of trees, rocks, and water. It might not be too much of a stretch of the imagination to think that Fujitarō walked into the woods and mountains of the Pacific Northwest and felt a strong resonance.

There was something familiar about the scene that must have given him a lot of inspiration. I see Fujitarō as a very sensitive, creative, and expressive artist who felt the full impact of the natural beauty and was not afraid to embrace it and use it. Which, it turns out, is the very essence of how Japanese gardens are created.

STONE IS USED THROUGHOUT KUBOTA GARDEN. You have to really pay attention to find some of the stones. Others sit prominently and majestically. Some you don't even notice because they seem so natural and in place, while others, although quiet, make strong statements.

These stones punctuate different areas of the garden; they work as anchors to other elements of the garden; and they bring a refined, yet untamed sensation to the garden. Although the garden is well maintained, the presence of stones in some places brings the feeling of walking in the mountains.

Fujitarō Kubota followed the tradition of using stone as the structural framework of the garden. The Japanese garden within Kubota Garden has a more typical use of stone and water. The aim was not to show individuality or expression as much as to elicit calm and serenity. Here he stuck more to the traditional use of stone. This was one of the first things Fujitarō built on the property sometime in the Twenties. The stroll garden also has some great stones. It uses large, mostly flat-top stones and aims to fill the visitor with equanimity and peace. The way the stones are used here lets you forget how big the stones really are. They are placed as if the entire garden grew around them, instead of them being placed later according to the design.

And one cannot forget the waterfall. The use of stone in the waterfall is impressive, bold, yet sensitive. The size of the fall is amazing, and the stones are very energetic. Many of them stand, lean, and have a lot of movement, giving the observer the sensation of being deep in the mountains and forest. The construction of this waterfall must have been a massive undertaking. I cannot help but sense the artistic flair of Fujitarō in this work. He must have had a very clear vision and determination. Stones tell the story.

Before Fujitarō Kubota and several other Japanese gardeners put down roots in the Pacific Northwest, stone use in a garden was unheard of. Stones were just stones, material for bulkheads and retaining walls, not unique and powerful design elements as we understand them today. They were useful, but no one thought of drawing attention to them.

FACING Kubota Garden Renton Avenue rockery from entry drive, circa 1930s.

At the beginning, Fujitarō had a very hard time finding stones. He would look for them in farmlands and alongside road construction. The farmers and construction workers were happy to get rid of the stones. They must have wondered what in the world drove this landscaper to want to haul away their stones!

Then Fujitarō acquired a small plot in the hills to collect stones and hauled them from there until he ran out of reasonably sized stones. Again, he struggled to find stone.

Around the Sixties, Fujitarō started to work with local lumber companies that had access to trucks and grappling cranes and worked in the mountains. Fujitarō would ask them to bring stones from the mountains when they were up there collecting logs. Some of those companies began to use more and more of their truck beds for stones instead of lumber. They began to specialize in stones over time, switching entirely from their lumber business to the stone business.

Fujitarō did not use stones in his clients' gardens right away. At first, he created more Western-style gardens. But gradually he used more and more stone until it became his signature style. His use of stone set him apart from many other gardeners, and this attracted many younger gardeners to come work with him. These younger gardeners would start their own business after being trained by Fujitarō.

I often wonder, before Fujitarō came to be known for using stone in his design, how did a conversation with a client go?

"You want to bring a big *what* into my backyard?"

Now, there is a general acceptance and even expectation of stone use in landscape, regardless of the size of the garden. If the use of stone were just a novelty or a mere fad, it would have died out already. However, the use of stone is everywhere, not only in gardens, but in other spaces as well. This shows that the use of stone taps into something deeper, something more universal. Architects, landscapers, and garden designers all found a new and powerful design element in stone.

FACING Fujitarō Kubota and assistants placing stones, Seattle University, 1965.

Kubota Garden: A Zen Sketch

Charles Johnson

IT WAS THE END of the day at a private high school in Burien. Seventeen-year-old Joshua Davis was in the locker room, changing out of his sweats—Coach Williams had his class run around the track five times before soccer practice—and Joshua was putting on his street clothes when he heard the voice of Eli Jenson behind him.

"Hey, Joshua," he said. "Why don't you cut off those dreadlocks? You'd see the ball better if they weren't swinging in your face."

Joshua felt his stomach clench and his lungs tighten, but he ignored Eli. He didn't want trouble. He just wanted to go home after a long day at school. But Eli was always messing with him, flipping him off, and pulling his chain.

"Did you hear me?" said Eli, stepping closer. "Those stringy dreads make you look like that monster Miss Cummings talked about in our mythology class. What's her name? Medusa. And you know you're ugly enough already!"

Then Eli grabbed a fistful of Joshua's dreads and pulled on them from behind, painfully snapping back his head. Right then, Joshua was on him like white on rice. Pounding on Eli with a flurry of punches and in an elixir of rage and hatred that frightened even Joshua himself. Blossoms of blood spread on his knuckles. And, as luck would have it, at just that moment, Coach Williams came into the locker room. He pulled the boys apart, yelling that he wouldn't tolerate fighting in his gym. Then he hauled Joshua and Eli to the principal's office. And *he*, furious and red-faced and puffing up like a blowfish, chewed their fat good and suspended both boys for a day.

Now, the last thing Joshua wanted to do was go home to face his parents. They weren't wealthy, but they scrimped and saved to keep him in a private school and away from kids they saw as being a bad influence. He knew they didn't want him to be just another sad statistic. Or funneled into the school-to-prison pipeline. So far their gamble was paying off. His teachers liked him, and he was doing well, academically, even though he often felt lonely, because he was one of only five black students in what felt sometimes like a vanilla sea of well-off, privileged kids so different in their backgrounds from his own. A couple were his friends in the chess club, and on the school newspaper, where he sometimes published one of his poems.

But after school, as he walked slowly along Renton Avenue South, his neck hurting, and still wound up way too tight, Joshua wondered for the hundredth time where he belonged. Or if he belonged anywhere. At school, he felt self-conscious and lost. His counselor, Mrs. Davis, noticed this and said to him, "Joshua, I've noticed that you're always pretty relaxed, but you never *completely* relax." He got silent when she said that because it was true—he never let down his guard. At school, he never relaxed completely, and he knew he didn't have the luxury of clowning around like the other kids, because his parents had already given him the Talk every young black male one day has to receive.

His father told him that if the other kids went into the bathroom to drink or do a little dope, that was fine for them, but if *he* did those things and got caught messing up in a country like America, with its double standards for whites and people of color, his punishment would be far more severe than it would be for them. And if he ever went to jail, they didn't have the money or connections to bribe a judge to bail him out. So, no. He knew he didn't have the luxury of making mistakes. Or completely relaxing when he stepped outside his parents' home. And back in the 'hood, he had to be careful not to sound too bookish or nerdy around other kids. Before saying anything, he had to quickly think before he spoke, selecting his words as carefully as a poet might, so people wouldn't think he was putting on airs by using words, phrases, or ideas they didn't know. In both worlds he straddled, Joshua felt like an outsider. Or someone on a tightrope. It was as if he wore a mask at school and another one in the 'hood. Walking home, he felt a twinge of anger at everything that moved. He trembled at the thought of what he might have done to Eli. And almost every day he wondered: Who am I? What am I? How can I survive, feeling split in half this way?

No, he didn't want to tell his parents he'd been kicked out of school. His family had lived in Rainier Beach for less than a year, so parts of the neighborhood were still new for him, like the road he only now noticed snaking away from the street. At its entrance there was a big rock outlined in gold by late afternoon light. It was engraved with Japanese characters, and below them the words Kubota Garden. Curious, he let his feet carry him eastward toward the entrance. With each step away from Renton Avenue, as he moved closer to the garden's welcoming gate, the world seemed to grow quieter the way he felt whenever he entered a sacred place like his parents' church, with the noise of traffic and city sounds being replaced by a hymnal stillness. In a similar way, with each step he took toward the garden, the constant background static and congestion of his thoughts, the obsessive memories and fears, hopes and desires—*that* inner racket began to fade away like puffs of smoke scattered by the most gentle of breezes.

As he picked up a few pamphlets inside the entry gate on the history of the garden, he noticed how there were brilliant Japanese maples and madronas, and new still-blond pines that seemed chiseled out of air all around him. That made the air he inhaled so oxygen-rich the space behind his eyes and between his ears begin to feel clearer, less tight, and he remembered something said by his science teacher Mr. Smith: One acre of forest absorbed six tons of carbon dioxide and put out four tons of oxygen, which was enough to meet the needs of eighteen people.

Inside the entrance now, he saw a sign inviting him to strike a bronze bell, and he did so, the sound vibrating in the cavity of his chest. Then he saw paths winding away to his left and right. Which one to choose? Joshua wasn't sure so he just went to the left, uncertain of what might be ahead. But after only a few seconds of walking on a path of leaf-filtered light designed to simultaneously conceal and reveal Nature's generosity, he emerged from a section of forest into an opening that made him stop and stare. Just stare, for he had fallen into what could only be called a sensuous poem and a profound mystery, and at its center was a large spirit stone. Its density, the heaviness of it, seemed to bend space and time around itself. He stood silently before it, forced by its presence to listen since he was unexpectedly part of a vignette of stone, emptiness, water, plants and... Joshua. The rough stone, with its tonsured top and wide center, seemed to have its own personality and was the focal point and bone structure of the scene in which he found himself. It was probably hundreds of years old, older than America, very old, and held secrets Joshua felt he could not begin to imagine.

There were lessons to be learned here, he realized, and then he wondered, How had this forest, so different from the rest of Seattle and hiding in plain sight, come to be? Joshua let his heavy backpack slide off his shoulder to the ground and sat down by the stone. Others quietly visiting the garden gave him a friendly nod as they walked the paths. They were Vietnamese, Somalis, Filipinos, black Americans, whites and Latinos, slow walking and letting the twenty acres of forest bathe them with its spirit. He opened the pamphlet he picked up at the entrance and began to read a remarkable story he shamefully knew nothing about until now.

Long ago, or so he read, this place where he sat had been a stinking swamp, a waste area of tangled brush in Upper Rainier Beach. Mapes Creek coursed through it. No one believed the place had any value. Not until Fujitarō Kubota immigrated from the small Japanese island of Shikoku to Hawaii in 1907, from there to San Francisco, then up the coast to the sawmills in Selleck, and finally to Seattle, where he for a time managed hotels and apartment buildings in a segregated area that would one day become the International District. With his free time, he helped friends in the gardening business, discovered this sort of work brought him both pleasure and peace, and in 1923 founded the Kubota Gardening Company. When he looked at the five acres of swamp with the eyes of an artist, for Fujitarō was an amateur Kabuki actor, often taking the role of female characters, and was also a singer in the Japanese Gidayu tradition—when *those* eyes took in what so many others had ignored, he thought it would be perfect as a showcase for his nursery, a place to demonstrate to his clients the kinds of gardens he could create for them in the spirit of Buddhism and Konkōkyō, the branch of Shintoism he belonged to, one devoted to achieving spiritual awakening through the experience of nature. Draining the swamp required the hot work of digging a trench ten feet deep, but once that was done, he envisioned where he stood as a serene place for meditation where Japanese families and others prohibited from enjoying full citizenship in Seattle might find a retreat from worldly conflicts. A place that reconciled opposites, transcended the dualities that divided humankind and, most important of all, provided a Way or Dao for visitors to merge their hearts and minds with heaven and earth.

But then came World War II.

In 1942, Fujitarō and all members of his family were ordered to relocate to a concentration camp in Idaho. It was called the Minidoka War Relocation Center. Predictably, the camp was bleak, on barren desert land, and surrounded by an electrified barbed wire fence. Japanese citizens had to take loyalty oaths. Some became no-no boys by refusing to answer the last two questions about loyalty and serving in the military, but Fujitarō's two sons, Tak and Tommy, decided to become translators and instructors in the army. And he, based on his work in Seattle, became the camp's chief gardener in charge of beautification projects. Even though he suffered greatly during his three years of internment, Fujitarō created an entrance garden that featured an Honor Roll board for the 418 Japanese Americans who left their families in Minidoka to serve in the U.S. military,

as his sons had done. Today that concentration-camp garden is the site for a yearly pilgrimage for those who want to learn about this dark chapter in America's history.

Joshua read next about Kubota's return to Seattle in 1945. When he saw what remained of his original garden, his eyes burned with tears. Weeds choked the roads. The once beautiful ponds were filled with trash, effluvium, and the stench of swamp water. Yet—and yet—those three years of neglect suggested to Kubota's artistic eyes the possibility for something unique, spontaneous, and with a touch of serendipity a traditional Japanese garden did not possess. Never trained in Japan in the time-honored ways of gardening there (the old masters refused to share their secrets with him), and never one to work with a pre-established blueprint, but instead someone conditioned by Shintoism and Zen to listen to nature, Fujitarō saw how the wild growth uncultivated and bursting with variety might complement and complete the delicate order conceived by his own spirit and sensibility. Nature and mind *could* balance each other like yin and yang.

Using a scythe, he cut away weeds high as his waist, but of course they weren't all *that* high because Fujitarō was only four feet, eleven inches tall. Yet his spirit was expansive, and by virtue of that the garden expanded to the twenty-plus acres in which Joshua found himself.

He slipped the pamphlet about the garden into his backpack. Slowly, a thought burst to the surface of Joshua's mind, like koi fish breaking the surface of the garden's ponds: There could be no beauty without ugliness. No success without failure. No pleasure without pain, or life without death. These twins were forever linked like sunlight and shade. Something in Joshua began to relax. His thoughts drifted to the internment camp in Idaho. Slavery a century before was an unspeakable evil for his ancestors. And racial segregation a seventy-year violation of everything this country said it stood for. But Kubota—an outsider as Joshua felt himself to be—had not given up hope, despite the fact that in 1927 he was not a naturalized American citizen, and therefore could not buy those first five acres of land. So he had a friend secure the land for him. Joshua saw that once the obstacles were overcome, Kubota's deeds spread seeds of beauty that flowered as far away as the Seattle Center, the Japanese Garden at Bloedel Reserve, the Rainier Club, and at Seattle University. He, once excluded, let anyone come to his ever-changing garden. That Joshua found fascinating, because it seemed to suggest that, like the neglected garden during the war years, America's swamp of social injustice was strangely enough the precondition for creating people of color determined to act in a generous spirit exactly opposite that of those who oppressed them.

As he walked slowly, letting the forest paths of gravel and stone guide his feet, that old, nagging feeling of himself separated from others began to fall away from him, and he felt just maybe he *could* return hate with love, and meanness with kindness as Kubota did. But he felt something more, too. The bright, translucent air was so oxygenated his attention focused now on his breaths, how each was different, never the same as the last one. Some shallow, some deep, some warm, some cool, with every in-breath or exhale fresh and new. For Kubota's garden awakened him to the fact that he was essentially and inescapably a body among so many other bodies—cherry blossoms that still held the plangent knoll of the bell he'd struck, lanterns, bridges, hedges, shrubs, and the miraculous gift of far-reaching trees that were colossi towering above him. This felt like a spiritualized sensuality, because walking these acres was an aerobic experience that had him suddenly descending slopes on steps made of rocks, and climbing hills that did not so much rise as they sheered skyward in rippling planes, and so he had to place his feet down ever so carefully if he didn't want to slip or fall, and that let him feel with every footfall the firmness of the earth meeting and pressing back to balance each of his movements. It was strange to say, maybe even to *think*, but it felt to Joshua that everything that was and ever had been was here. Always changing form, but here, nevertheless.

He moved on through Kubota's work of art, made of what he was made, finding and losing himself at the same time in the rhythms of emptiness and forms. Through the Fera Fera Forest, the Tom Kubota Stroll Garden, the Japanese Garden with its Kasuga stone lantern, and the Moon Bridge that represented in a wizardly light how hard it is to lead a good life with the words, "Hard to walk up and hard to walk down." Joshua realized he was the tiniest of figures blending into this picture, beneath a canopy of empty sky that seemed endless, growing darker now as night came on. Feeling a little winded, breathing high in his lungs, he sat down on a bench near a fossil stone forty million years old, just below a waterfall and near a pond. Whatever feelings of anger and fear that had overwhelmed him thinned and disappeared, as if they never were. Eli Jenson's taunts were as far removed from his mind as the man in the moon.

Quietly, he sat, breathing slowly, letting his guard down, dropping deeper into his embodiment, feeling as if his fight earlier happened in another life, or to someone else—someone he no longer was, or certainly was not at this moment. Every moment was different in the garden. And so was he. Right here, right now he was the spill of early evening light on delicate leaves lighter than a whisper, the sinewy bark of trees which reminded him of the wrinkled skin of elephants, the breeze feathering pond water into ripples, the muffled brooling of the waterfall Kubota had created, the water flowing freely, formless, and capable of assuming the shape of anything. Joshua felt he could do that now, for in just this past hour the garden had nourished his spirit, showing him the littleness of what people called "race" in the vastness of Being. That made him smile because he, so aware of his body now, knew that one day he would come back to this place, this Earth, like a raindrop falling back into the sea, and nourish it as it did him now.

And underneath it all, *underneath it all,* he could hear the garden whisper gently that he would never die.

He pulled his cellphone from his backpack and checked the time. Eight pm. It was finally time to leave this place where he felt he fit so well and go home. To face his parents. He wasn't going to fool himself about how they would react to his day's suspension. He knew they would go ballistic as the numinous garden lingered in his mind. And that was all right. That thought no longer frightened him.

Nothing did.

Silence, Stone, Reflection

Nathan Wirth

精神

Kubota Garden

i.m. Jim Thwing, 1929 – 2002

To learn what's behind
the character for
forgiveness, you have only
to walk these paths & imagine
yourself a brush wielded
by someone who knew the truth
of the *Analects*: that one
who loves mountains
loves kindness, that one
who loves water
loves wisdom. Bamboo,
cherry, Japanese
maple & pines all mingle
with Oregon grape, salal, deer
fern, wild rhododendron.
Listen: that isn't wind keening

through barbed-wire
or sagebrush, but is only
the sound of air & water
shaping stone along
with the shuffling
of your own feet
responding to the gift
the world is, saying
yes   thank you   yes

SAMUEL GREEN

Kubota's Garden Spirits

Jason M. Wirth

VISITORS TO KUBOTA GARDEN sense that as beautiful as it is, the garden is more than aesthetically pleasing. It somehow feels like a spiritual place, the garden as a temple of nature where the human world and spirit world touch each other. The mindfully arranged stones and waters, the pruned trees, the seasonal transformations, even the historical accidents (parts of Kubota's nursery that were later incorporated into the garden, pre-contact trees that were not removed, etc.), awaken visitors from the banalities and stresses of daily life and attune them to the spiritual dimensions of the natural world.

The words "spirit" and "spiritual" are so overused, however, that they are on the brink of meaning everything and nothing. Yet one is nonetheless compelled to try and articulate precisely what one means by drawing attention to this aspect of the garden. In my conversation with Linda Kubota Byrd,[1] granddaughter of Fujitarō Kubota and daughter of Tom Kubota, she suggested that to "experience the spirit of the garden, people must stop the chatter and merge with the subtle energy, to feel it in their bodies, rather than just see it with their eyes." Moreover, one cannot cede the ground to vague platitudes about the spirituality of the Earth. How exactly does one dwell among Kubota's Garden Spirits?

We can begin with an elemental insight from the *Sakuteiki* (*The Garden Making Record*), the Heian-period classic and perhaps the oldest extant book on gardening in the world. As we also see embellished in the essay by Kentaro Kojima in this book, the vitality of stone and its relationship to water are critical. The *Sakuteiki* counsels the garden architect to learn to *listen* to the stones and follow their "desires." In a section called the "Secret Teachings on Setting Stones," we are instructed to "choose a particularly splendid stone and set it as the Main Stone. Then, following the request of the first stone, set others accordingly."[2]

How does one hear a stone's request? Fujitarō Kubota's capacity to do so not only attuned him to the spiritual ground of Japanese gardening, but it also forms the living structure of the garden itself. He was a regional pioneer in introducing the usage of stone, and Kubota Garden is full of dramatic stone personalities—"spirit stones" as he sometimes called them. To a casual observer, stones epitomize the dull inertia of the earth. They appear utterly still, obdurate, hopelessly opaque. In this way, they are good examples of what Japanese Buddhists call "form." Stones change so slowly that they are ready figures of the almost imperceptibly slow pace of change on a geological scale. Yet they move! Even stones, masters of holding to their form, are also what the Buddhists call "empty" or *kū* (空). They are not just stones all by themselves, but they are interrelated and implicated with the movement and vitality of all things. When the *Heart Sutra*, the pith of Mahāyāna Buddhist practice, claims that "form is emptiness and emptiness is form," it is counseling us to become aware of their mutual reliance. Yes, a stone is a stone, but it is not just a stone. Emptiness is often associated with water, which has no form of its own, but which can take the shape of any form. Listening to stone is the capacity to detect the mutual interdependence of its form and emptiness. As an old Zen adage teaches, "the mountains are always walking."

A Gathering of *Kami* in the Garden

Such considerations, while deeply at play in Kubota Garden, are nonetheless generally true of most Japanese garden design. Fujitarō Kubota was also an experimenter, and his design discoveries and intuitions enhanced the ancient traditions upon which he relied. How might one construe some of the unusual, even singular, ways that Fujitarō Kubota staged the nourishing and healing energies in his garden?

When one climbs to the top of the falls and discovers the spot where Fujitarō and his wife meditated and greeted the rising sun, our sense that this is a spiritual place is further confirmed. Near the meditation benches, there is a striking prayer stone with the *Tenchi Kakitsuke* (Heaven

and Earth's Reminder, often called "the Divine Reminder") inscribed in Japanese. This is the central and most important prayer for Konkōkyō (金光教, the Golden Light Teachings), to which Linda Kubota Byrd confirmed that her grandfather was a "devout" practitioner. It was his "source of inspiration." He even had a custom-built Konkōkyō altar in his house that Linda remembers as "elegant in its simplicity." Konkōkyō is a relatively new form of ancient Japanese Shinto and Buddhist animistic practices. It was founded in 1859 in the rural farming communities in what is today Okayama Prefecture by Bunjirō Kawate (1814–1883), who received the name Ikigami Konkō Daijin, a title that means the "living spirit (*kami*), Divine Mediator of the Universe."

Konkōkyō still voluntarily accepts its characterization as a form of non-state or sectarian Shinto. The kanji for the word "Shinto" are made up of the Chinese pronunciation (*shin*) of the graph for *kami* (神), the indwelling earth spirits, and *dō*, the Japanese reading of a graph that English speaking readers know better in its original Chinese pronunciation: *Dao* (道), the Way of all things. Shinto, or *kami no michi* in a Japanese reading, is the Way of the *kami*. It is to awaken to and cultivate the indwelling spiritual dimension of the natural world. In this respect, we could think of Kubota Garden as the gathering and intensification of the *kami*. Linda thought that not only is the garden "peaceful" and a respite from the "hustle-bustle" of the everyday, but that it "re-energizes" one.

Although Konkōkyō ministers still wear the white robes typical of Shinto practices, the religion has some distinctive and sometimes unique practices. It did not originally emphasize the Shinto *kami* over Buddhist Bodhisattvas (enlightened beings). *Kami* and Bodhisattvas both comprised the indwelling earth energies and spirits. (Such practices in Konkōkyō and other new religions are sometimes called *Shinbutsu-shūgō*, a syncretism of Shinto and Buddhism.) In this respect, it is worth noting that Konkōkyō espouses respect for all spiritual practices and explicitly does not require Konkōkyō practitioners to renounce other practices. In a Konkōkyō Scripture, we are admonished to respect "all religions": "Your faith should not be narrow, it should be broad."[3] It is narrow both to discriminate against other religions and to follow a single religion obsessively. This is not to think broadly about the world.[4]

Konkōkyō also emphasizes the role of the mediator, link, or go-between that intercedes between the spirit and earthly realm on behalf of practitioners—indeed they are ultimately the same realm. It also introduces a great *kami* not found in earlier forms of Shinto: the Great Parent Spirit, Tenchi Kane no Kami (the Great Parent Kami of Heaven and Earth). This is the Great Spirit that is the unity of heaven and earth, the spirit of all spirits (similar to what some indigenous peoples call the Great Spirit), the life force of all beings in the universe. This is the *kami* that

FACING Procession at Tak Kubota and Kiyo Kaneko's wedding, 1940.

not only manifests as all of the individual *kami* and bodhisattvas, but also as all of the evolving and interrelated things that compose the universe. For this reason, Konkōkyō, unlike traditional Shinto, does not enshrine individual deities. The whole earth is the Divine Spirit's shrine.

In calling the Parent Spirit "Tenchi," literally "heaven and earth," Konkōkyō does not banish the Parent Spirit to an otherworldly dimension. Tenchi is sometimes translated in English language Konkōkyō literature as the "universe," for there is no being and no place that it excludes. Just as all beings are composed of and united through their underlying energy, the Parent Spirit is both energy and all beings. One might even say that Tenchi is the "multiverse" in order to speak of all beings with maximal inclusivity. Yet simply thinking of Tenchi as the "multiverse" risks obscuring its spiritual dimension. This does not mean, however, that we should confuse "heaven (*ten*, 天)" with an otherworldly dimension. Konkōkyō does not believe in an afterlife in which the righteous dwell in the bliss of heaven and the sinners suffer the endless torments of hell. After death, we return to the energy from which we emerged.[5] The phrase Tenchi emerges from Classical Chinese philosophy and culture, where it was both prevalent and indispensible. Tenchi (天地) is the multiverse as both energy and its manifestations, the spiritual and its natural forms, Dao and all beings, even emptiness and form in the Buddhist sense above. Although heaven and earth are opposites (like yin and yang or emptiness and form), they are inseparable, interdependent, and mutually reliant. The supreme spiritual challenge is to activate their non-duality, to align oneself *within* and *as* the circulation of heaven and earth.

The Konkōkyō practitioner is therefore called to awaken the spirit or *kami* (神) within herself and within all beings by appealing to Konkō Daijin's mediation or channeling of the Great Parent, Tenchi Kane no Kami. Hence, their most important prayer, Tenchi Kakitsuke, first distributed in handwritten copies by Konkō Daijin in 1873, calls for the awakening and attunement of one's heart to the great Earth spirit through the mediation of Konkō Daijin and his successors. The Tenchi Kakitsuke, found at the center of all Konkōkyō altars and inscribed on Fujitarō Kubota's prayer stone, reads:

> Through Ikigami Konkō Daijin
> To Tenchi Kane no Kami,
> Pray with a single heart.
> The divine favor depends
> On your own heart
> On this very day, pray.[6]

FACING Detail of Prayer Stone *(left)*; Prayer Stone on top of the Mountainside *(right)*.

116

The kanji being translated as heart, *shin* or *kokoro* (心), means the heart and mind and their interrelationship. To have or even *be* a single heart, *isshin* (一心), is to align one's own heart-mind with the heart-mind of the Great Parent Spirit through the helpful mediation of the heart-mind of Konkō Daijin and his successors. It is the alignment of one's own heart and mind with heaven and earth. Tenchi Kane no Kami is not some remote god and should not be approached in an otherworldly way. Kami Sama, as Tenchi Kane no Kami is sometimes affectionately addressed, is the universe's ever circulating and genetic energies. It is the Way or Dao of all things. One does not pray to Kami Sama as some remote and hopefully benevolent being. One attempts rather to align one's whole heart-mind (*kokoro*) with the Way of all things. If Kami Sama is remote, Kami Sama is powerless, ineffectual, and even irrelevant.

The relationship between Kami Sama and human beings is mutually interdependent (*aiyo kakeyo*) and mutually reliant: by awakening to Kami Sama, the forces and energies of heaven and earth vitalize. Human vitality for its part realizes itself through Kami Sama. In a sense, the awakened human heart and mind manifests the alignment, mutual interdependence, and co-awakening of heaven and earth. They are awake and alive together or not at all. Hence Konkōkyō teaches the mutual reciprocity of heaven and earth, spirit and nature, Kami Sama and the practitioner (*ujiko*): "because of the practitioner there is Kami and because of Kami there is the practitioner." An old manual of Konkōkyō Scriptures explained the importance of *aiyo kakeyo,* or mutual reliance, by comparing it to the workings of the human body: "From the working of the limbs and the five sensory organs to the functioning of the cells—everything is bound together and unified solely by this relation. The same is true of the mutual relations of all things in the universe."[7] And what is a garden if not mutual reliance between the gardener and the earth, drawing out and bringing into mutual relief the earthly and spiritual dimensions? A good gardener does not seek to dominate the earth but rather cooperate with it, allowing each to become itself through this mutual interaction.

Konkō Daijin is not therefore best understood as a prophet or as somehow more than human. He embodies, as did the Buddha in his own way, the realization of what we all fundamentally are if we can find a way to awaken our hearts and minds. The Konkōkyō process of awakening relies on mediation, which Konkō Daijin introduced to the Japanese Shinto and Buddhist heritage. *Toritsugi* is mediating or channeling heaven and earth, Kami Sama and humanity, linking them together in the theater of the heart-mind. As the reality of climate change and the ecological crisis more broadly becomes more and more apparent, we can take solace and inspiration from the way that Kubota Garden manifests a different relationship to the earth. Konkōkyō was born among farmers who worked the earth and it strives, despite our inability to always get what we prefer, to be grateful for all that we have. All things great and small are regarded as gifts. We give ourselves over to heaven and earth and participate in its mutual reliance with our efforts. The garden epitomizes this mutually beneficial relationship.

It is also important to emphasize that this mutual reliance is rooted in the vitality and creativity of the earth. In the Scripture called *The Teachings of the Way* (*Michi Oshie no Taiko*), we are told to "commit all things to heaven and depend on earth"[8] and not to "defile any part of Kami's earth without reason."[9] This commitment attunes us to the mysterious life of the things of the earth, a life that we could already see in the paradoxical vitality of stone. "The things of heaven and earth cannot be known through the eye; they can only be looked upon in wonder."[10] In the Scriptures on Prohibitions, we are reminded not to "be thankful to heaven, but to be ignorant of one's debt to earth."[11] In another scripture we are counseled that if we want to see Kami, "step outside the door of the house. The sky above you and the earth beneath you is Kami."[12] The garden expresses this realization.

In the end, it is also important not to get too caught up in the technicalities of Konkōkyō and lose contact with the visceral manifestation of Kubota Garden's spiritual dimension. This experience has nothing to do with believing in a particular religion. It certainly does not require understanding the letter of Konkōkyō or even being able to detect its presence in the garden. Linda remembers that her grandfather would just sit and contemplate a potential gardening site as if he were "communing" with it. He would not produce or rely on blueprints or plans. He would not ask for money in advance. He would just wait for the place to "speak" to him.

This was already the case when he first found the generally maligned wetland area in Upper Rainier Beach, with Mapes Creek running through it, that would one day become Kubota Garden. (He would have to dig a trench ten feet deep to channel the creek.) Linda had the sense that

INSET The Konkō Church of Seattle (1713 S. Main Street). It was founded in 1928, the year after Kubota purchased the first parcel that was to become Kubota Garden. The church moved to its present location in 1936. It is one of fourteen such churches in North America. Twelve of them are on the West Coast and two are in Chicago and Toronto.

he could see that "this is it!" It was "like the land spoke to him. He must have had the vision of the whole garden from the beginning." Where some saw waste, Kubota intuited gold. Thomas Robinson in his 1992 thesis on the garden characterized this movement from listening to the land to responding to its desires as "Passive Attitude followed by Dynamic Action."[13] In some sense, one could even say that Kubota had the eye and heart to be able to mediate the land, vitalizing its relationship between heaven and earth.

Kubota Garden and its spirits leave us with some important lessons. Fujitarō Kubota, in part for linguistic reasons, did not extend his Konkōkyō practice to his children or grandchildren. This is not to say that its vital impulse was lost on them. Linda reflected that her father, Tom Kubota, the garden's "humble unsung hero," was "Konkōkyō without the label." She also sees this in herself: "Even though I didn't have a name for my personal relationship with spirit, as I've come to learn about Konkōkyō, I realize that I have unknowingly shared the same beliefs as my grandfather." The garden nourishes and heals because it channels a kind of archaic earth awakening.

A Relentlessly Generous Mind and Heart

Fujitarō himself never received a full classical training in Japanese garden design. Access to such education was often strictly controlled. Although he returned to Japan three times to study, he could only get so far because, as he recalled in 1973, it is "taught in the rigid old family system."[14] Whenever he got stuck and did not know what to do, he "went into the woods and prayed to Kami for help." Linda recalls that her grandfather would always respond to hardship by claiming that "Kami will take care of this." Gardening is not only the proactive art of design, it is also listening, letting be, respecting the way of things, and attuning to the emerging personality of a place.

Konkō Daijin knew much personal hardship, and he lived in an agricultural community that also knew it intimately. Fujitarō and his family also knew plenty of suffering (the crushing psychic violence of white supremacy, incarceration in Minidoka, the legal prohibition against owning land, financial hardships, and the many challenges of human life). The Konkō Church of Seattle was itself shut down during the war and did not open again until 1956. Pain can make one small and broken, bitter and resentful. Yet the opposite was the case. "Your heart-mind can help you to live, or it can destroy you"[15] says a passage from the Scripture called *Instructions Concerning the Faith* (*Shinjin no Kokoroe*). Linda recalls that her grandfather and father never complained about what had happened during the war. Their response was, rather, to create this garden, an expression of their grateful, appreciative, and relentlessly generous minds and hearts.

The Kubota family, and those inspired to protect and promote their vision, worked hard. Not far from the Prayer Stone one finds the 1962 Memorial Stone. On its backside one finds a simple history of Fujitarō Kubota written by the Reverend Fumio Matsui, the first head minister of the resurrected Konkō Church of Seattle.[16] Its history of Fujitarō Kubota recounts that "with his own hands he cleared the land, dug several ponds, and cut the trees to build the garden. Mr. Kubota studied landscaping, suffered hard work and put great effort into this project." In the *Gorikai* Scripture of Konkōkyō, we find the following words that also aptly describe Fujitarō, Tom, and the many other members of the Kubota family as well as those who strive to protect and enhance their legacy: "When the children of Kami are climbing a ten-mile hill, they must not take it easy even when they have gone nine and a half miles… To relax one's efforts is to go backward to the place of beginning."[17]

Endnotes

1 Byrd, Linda Kubota (interview, September 23, 2018).

2 *Sakuteiki: Visions of the Japanese Garden* (2001) Translated by Jirō Takei and Marc P. Keane (Tuttle Publishing) 184.

3 Schneider, Delwin B. (1962) *Konkōkyō: A Japanese Religion* (The International Institute for the Study of Religion) 88.

4 Voice of the Universe #15, Gorikai II Ichimura II Mitsuguro 17 – 2.

5 The Church teaches that Tenchi Kane No Kami does not only take care of the living, but the dead also remain under Kami's care. The soul returns to Kami's eternal care while the body returns to the earth and remains in its care (see II Kashiwabara Toku 5).

6 Ikigami Konkō Daijin, Tenchi Kane no Kami (生神金光大神, 天地金乃神), Isshin ni negae (一心に願). Okage wa waga kokoro ni ari (おかげは和賀心にあり). Kongetsu konnichi de tanomei (今月今日でたのめい).

7 Konkōkyō Hombu (Headquarters of Konkōkyō) (1933). *The Sacred Scriptures of Konkōkyō.* Konkō-cho, xxxi.

8 Schneider, 83.

9 Ibid.

10 Ibid, 84.

11 Ibid, 82.

12 Ibid, 88.

13 Robinson, Thomas M. (1992) *Traditions in Translation: The Gardens of Fujitarō Kubota* (Master's thesis in Landscape Architecture, University of Washington, 109.

14 Ito, Kazuo (1973) *Issei: A History of Japanese Immigrants in North America* (Japanese Community Service) 860.

15 Schneider, 85.

16 The founding head minister was the Rev. Rikimatsu Hideshima. After the Rev. Matsui resigned in 1966, the Rev. Michihiro Yuasa was head minister for over fifty years. As of 2018, the new head minister is the Rev. Robert Giulietti, who runs the church with his wife, the Rev. Mitsue Kusuki Giulietti.

17 Schneider, 98.

生神　金光　大神

天地金乃神　一心願

おかげは和賀心にあり

今月今日でたのめい

Through Ikigami Konko Daijin,
To Tenchi Kane No Kami,
Pray with a single heart.
The divine favor depends upon one's own heart.
On this very day pray.

精神

There Is Freedom
in the Garden

the turtles (too) are sacred
the slow of them mirrored alongside
ripples of water

all the humans pebbles
all the humans pebbling what it means to   go slow
all the humans gesturing (to each other)   community

& the trees (there)
lean upon themselves like   rest
lean upon themselves like   elders
lean upon themselves like   free

ANASTACIA-RENEÉ

追放
exile

Minidoka's Chief Gardener

Anna Tamura

FOLLOWING THE BOMBING of Pearl Harbor and entrance of the United States into World War II, President Franklin D. Roosevelt signed Executive Order 9066 in February 1942, which led to the mass roundup and incarceration of Japanese Americans from the West Coast. Fujitarō Kubota and his family were among the 110,000 West Coast Nikkei (Japanese Americans and legal residents of Japanese ancestry) to be forcibly removed from their homes and incarcerated in government-operated concentration camps. It was at the Minidoka camp in the Idaho desert where the Kubotas and other Seattle Nikkei spent the war years anxiously awaiting an unknown future. When the government at Minidoka needed a leader for improving the camp conditions, Fujitarō Kubota was chosen as Minidoka's chief gardener. Kubota went on to lead several "camp beautification" projects that resulted in profound and positive effects for his fellow Nikkei.

Prior to their forced removal from Seattle, the Kubotas were issued alien registration numbers 2767738 for Fujitarō and 2767737 for Kumae, and then issued family number 43186. In the spring of 1942, the Kubotas were sent to the Puyallup Assembly Center, named Camp Harmony. At Puyallup, horse stalls were hastily converted into living quarters, and Nikkei were required to adjust quickly to communal life under guard. It was during their time at Camp

Harmony that the Minidoka site was selected, and construction began on the camp. By the end of August 1942, Nikkei were being sent to Minidoka by train, five hundred at a time. Fujitarō, Kumae, and daughter May arrived at Minidoka on September 1, 1942 and were assigned to Block 26, Barrack 6, Room A. Block 26 was centrally located near the high school in the arc of residential blocks.

THE MINIDOKA RELOCATION CENTER was 33,000 acres of high desert land in south central Idaho, with an area of one thousand acres for the residential and developed area of the camp. The clearing of sagebrush, hasty construction of barracks, and large-scale disruption of the fragile soils created swirling dust clouds. Minidoka, which was to become the seventh-largest population center in Idaho during World War II, was still under construction when the Kubotas arrived. Surrounding the camp were miles of high desert sageland on one side and a deadly, swift flowing canal on the other. When the rains came in autumn, the dust turned to knee-deep mud between the barracks. In November 1942 after two months at Minidoka, the War Relocation Authority (WRA), the governing agency, announced the construction of the perimeter barbed-wire fence and guard towers. Aggravation, rage, widespread fear, and humiliation climaxed during a two-hour period in November 1942 when a contractor electrified the barbed wire fence. As temperatures plummeted and snow began to fall in December 1942, riots nearly ensued as coal had yet to arrive to heat the residential barracks. The psychological conditions were no better, as the stress of incarceration, uncertain future, and later a loyalty oath that divided families, friends, and communities contributed to an overall state of deep depression.

During that first year, these conditions led residents to immediately and increasingly call for improvements in the landscape. Individual Nikkei staked claim to the small areas around their barrack porches and between buildings. They transplanted and bonsaied sagebrush, planted small ornamental gardens, and dislodged and arranged the local lava rocks into Japanese-inspired gardens. The gardening activities paused during the Idaho winter and then began in earnest with the launch of a formal "beautification program" in early spring 1943.

WHEN MINIDOKA'S WRA OFFICIALS sought someone to lead the beautification program, they hired Fujitarō Kubota to be the chief gardener. Kubota was among many West Coast Nikkei who worked as landscape professionals in the pre-war period. They brought with them a deep knowledge of plants, Japanese cultural traditions, and a *gambatte* "don't give up" spirit that they adapted to the conditions of confinement. Throughout the ten camps scattered across the

FACING Fujitarō Kubota works with women on the garden next to the Block 26 barracks at Minidoka.

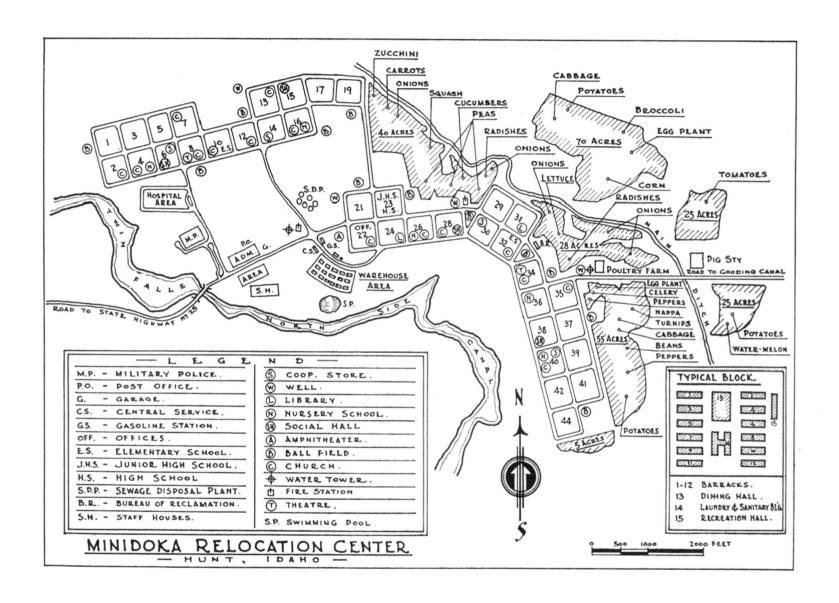

MINIDOKA RELOCATION CENTER
— HUNT, IDAHO —

LEGEND

M.P. — MILITARY POLICE.	S — COOP. STORE.
P.O. — POST OFFICE.	W — WELL.
G. — GARAGE.	L — LIBRARY.
C.S. — CENTRAL SERVICE.	N — NURSERY SCHOOL.
G.S. — GASOLINE STATION.	SH — SOCIAL HALL
OFF. — OFFICES.	A — AMPHITHEATER.
E.S. — ELEMENTARY SCHOOL.	B — BALL FIELD.
J.H.S. — JUNIOR HIGH SCHOOL.	C — CHURCH.
H.S. — HIGH SCHOOL.	⊕ — WATER TOWER.
S.D.P. — SEWAGE DISPOSAL PLANT.	🏛 — FIRE STATION
B.R. — BUREAU OF RECLAMATION.	T — THEATRE.
S.H. — STAFF HOUSES.	S.P. SWIMMING POOL

TYPICAL BLOCK

1-12 BARRACKS.
13 DINING HALL.
14 LAUNDRY & SANITARY BLDG.
15 RECREATION HALL.

Map labels: ZUCCHINI, CARROTS, ONIONS, SQUASH, CUCUMBERS, PEAS, RADISHES, CABBAGE, POTATOES, BROCCOLI, EGG PLANT, ONIONS, ONIONS, LETTUCE, RADISHES, CORN, ONIONS, TOMATOES, 40 ACRES, 70 ACRES, 25 ACRES, 28 ACRES, EGG PLANT, CELERY, PEPPERS, NAPPA, TURNIPS, CABBAGE, BEANS, PEPPERS, PIG STY, ROAD TO GOODING CANAL, 25 ACRES, POTATOES, WATER-MELON, 55 ACRES, POTATOES, 5 ACRES

HOSPITAL AREA, M.P., P.O., ADM., AREA, S.H., S.D.P., WAREHOUSE AREA, S.P., TWIN FALLS, ROAD TO STATE HIGHWAY № 25, NORTH SIDE CANAL, POULTRY FARM, MAIN DITCH

N · S

0 500 1000 2000 FEET

American West, they designed and built hundreds of landscape projects and gardens. Especially for Issei men, who had been stripped of their traditional leadership roles in camp, this activity was one mechanism where they could exert control over their circumstances and practice cultural traditions while soothing the daily, long-term stress created by the incarceration.

At Minidoka, the beautification program was initiated on a public scale in the spring of 1943. Kubota directed the planting of donated shade trees, shrubs, bulbs, and seeds from local Idahoans in Twin Falls.[1] Planting was based on a "carefully plotted landscaping plan" where shade trees were located at the corners of blocks to spatially define the boundaries of each block.[2] Elevated and rock-lined pathways between barracks, mess halls, and lavatory/laundry buildings were constructed to address the muddy conditions. The areas between barrack buildings were plowed to establish lawns and small vegetable plots known as victory gardens. Other large-scale projects included the construction of baseball fields, swimming holes, a nature preserve, and the conversion of thousands of acres of the sagebrush landscape into productive agricultural fields to support the camp population.

Kubota was involved in two landscape projects in Block 26. The first was a hothouse and nursery for trees, shrubs, and flowers that would be used for the duration of the war. It would eventually be six feet wide and eighty feet long, with the plants grown here intended for planting throughout the camp.[3] The second was a Japanese-style garden located adjacent to Barrack 6 and the mess hall; it contained basalt boulders, a pond, and carefully planted and tended trees and shrubs. The garden was surrounded by a low perimeter fence to demarcate its limits and became the backdrop for many family photographs due to the beautiful setting. Through these projects, Kubota helped foster the therapeutic and restorative powers of gardening, forging people-plant relationships and celebrating Japanese-style garden traditions, while also creating a sense of community and kindness.[4]

Fujitarō Kubota's most renowned and enduring work at Minidoka was the Japanese-style garden surrounding the Honor Roll at the camp's entrance. The garden project began in the spring of 1944 after the installation of the Honor Roll board in June 1943. The Honor Roll was fabricated

INSET *The Minidoka Irrigator*, April 10, 1943, with an article about the beautification program that mentions "Chief Gardener Kubota."

FACING Minidoka Relocation Center map.

and painted in the sign shop by artists Kenjirō Nomura and Kamekichi Tokita of Seattle. The Honor Roll originally listed the names of 418 Japanese Americans who had volunteered for the U.S. military from Minidoka while their families continued to be incarcerated at the camp. During the war, several hundred more men, and a handful of young women, entered military service, and their names were added. The Honor Roll and entrance garden were strategically placed just inside the only entrance to Minidoka so that after passing beneath the guard tower and through the gate, everyone entering the camp would see the overt symbols of patriotism and loyalty to the U.S.

Kubota's entrance garden was designed as a small sanctuary that integrated Japanese and American design tradition and aesthetics. The garden's design encouraged visitors to stop and visit, remember and admire the young people fighting for the United States, and then stroll and reflect within the garden setting. Enormous basalt boulders with special shapes and textures were carefully chosen from the surrounding desert and strategically placed throughout the garden. The boulders were individually chosen by Kubota and his crew on the outskirts of the camp where basalt outcroppings dotted the high desert scrub. The crew dislodged the boulders, transported them to the garden, and then Kubota personally directed the placement of the rocks. Mounds, stepping stones, and trees lined the garden's edge with shrubs and perennial flowers planted throughout.

As in Japanese garden design, the location and arrangements of landscape features and rocks are important components to the overall design, symbols that often convey an underlying meaning. In Kubota's Minidoka garden there are elements which may have complemented the overt patriotism displayed by the Honor Roll. One large mound was adjacent to the Honor Roll. This mound would have been viewed from the administration buildings, with the back of the Honor Roll forming the backdrop and blocking out the entrance buildings and gate. The placement and shapes of the rocks appear to mimic the silhouette of the eagle atop the Honor Roll. Another designed symbol may have been the construction of two straight pathways converging into the shape of a V for victory. These pathways contrasted with traditional Japanese garden design, where pathways are typically sinuous passageways. It is likely that Kubota designed the garden as it was being constructed, and thus we may never know his full design intentions. However, Kubota may have felt strongly attached to the Honor Roll and garden, as the names of his two sons, Takeshi and Tom, were listed on the central panel for their service in the U.S. military.

Kubota's landscape and nursery work at Minidoka had profound and restorative effects for his fellow imprisoned Nikkei, fostering community cohesion and empowerment. Kubota's gardens became destinations; his nursery-produced plants were distributed throughout the camp, and his work as head gardener led to developed and nurtured outdoor spaces throughout

FACING Kubota family Fujitarō, Kumae and May at Minidoka *(left)*. Fujitarō with two unidentified men *(right)*.

the camp. Kubota's landscape improvements were akin to healing agents that fostered a sense of empowerment, mental stability, and physical well-being. Through people-plant relationships, Kubota contributed to a sense of connectedness to the earth, the place, and the seasonal cycles. By cultivating harmony with Minidoka's environment of chaos and confusion, Kubota's work provided an opportunity for tranquility and instilled a sense of normalcy.

Fujitarō and Kumae departed Minidoka on March 23, 1945, to return to their home and business in Seattle. The government officially closed Minidoka on October 28, 1945. Minidoka's lands were partitioned into homesteads and given away in land lotteries in 1947 and 1949. Most of the residential areas, including Kubota's Block 26, were plowed under for agricultural lands and homesteads, though the entrance area to Minidoka was left intact and remained government land. In 1979, portions of the Minidoka site, including the entrance garden, were listed on the National Register of Historic Places. In 1988, President Reagan signed the Civil Liberties Act of 1988, which apologized to every living survivor on behalf of the nation and determined that the wartime incarceration was based on a long history of race prejudice, wartime hysteria, and a failure of political leadership. In 1990, Minidoka was dedicated as an Idaho Centennial Landmark. An article in the Twin Falls *Times-News* about the dedication noted, "The garden is hardly noticeable now. Filled and covered by the blowing dust and dry cheat grass, it looks like an odd mound with a few large rocks sticking out. It is a good place to stand for a better view of the surrounding countryside... But if one looks carefully beneath the brown grass, the carefully laid stone walkway leading to the garden can be seen."[5]

On January 17, 2001, Kubota's entrance garden was included in the presidential proclamation designating Minidoka as the 385th unit of the national park system to be preserved and interpreted for future generations. The designation spawned renewed interest in Kubota's entrance garden as the National Park Service took on management of the site. Kubota's entrance garden was documented, researched, and described in publications. In 2002, the National Park Service led an excavation of the garden, uncovering the V-shaped pathways and removing sixty years of soil that had settled on the site. A year later Kubota's garden became the ceremonial site of the annual Minidoka Pilgrimage. In 2011, the Honor Roll was re-established in its original location and the garden was linked to a loop trail for visitors to see and experience the many historic features at the site. A National Park Service visitor center was completed in 2019 with an interpretive film, park rangers, and a year-round presence at the site. Increasingly Kubota's garden at Minidoka will be visited by the American public and international visitors, just as Kubota Garden in Seattle is today.

FACING Japanese Americans looking at the camp's Honor Roll, a listing of all the Japanese Americans from the Minidoka concentration camp who volunteered for military service. Minidoka had the highest number of volunteers from the mainland United States.

Most descriptions of the Minidoka concentration camp focus on the cruelty of its tarpaper barracks, barbed-wire fences, and guard towers. However, the results of Fujitarō Kubota's work at Minidoka illustrate the agency with which Nikkei appropriated the camp landscape and actively transformed it into small yet distinct and important places of respite, respect, and beauty. This is evident in the design of the Honor Roll garden, steeped in irony and patriotic symbolism. Kubota's garden was forgotten and largely left untouched after the war, which resulted in its near pristine preservation. Today, the garden remains as his incarceration legacy, preserved by the same government that confined him. His garden is also the legacy of Japanese American action, ingenuity, strength, and place-making situated within a remote landscape evocative of racism and persecution—a forum for remembrance, healing, learning, and justice.

Disclaimer: The ideas and opinions expressed here are entirely my own and do not necessarily reflect those of the National Park Service.

Endnotes

1 "Beautification Program Underway in Project" (April 10. 1943) *The Minidoka Irrigator*, Vol. 3 No. 7.

2 Ibid.

3 "Experimental Nursery" (May 1, 1943) *The Minidoka Irrigator*.

4 Francis, Mark; Lindsey, Pat; Rice, Jay Stone, eds. (1994) *The Healing Dimensions of People-Plant Relations: Proceedings of a Research Symposium* (University of California, Davis).

5 Bowlin, Brad (May 27, 1990) "Dust-shrouded rock garden stirs memories" (Twin Falls *Times-News*).

Several publications and reports documented the garden. A selection of them includes: Burton, Jeffery F. Bergstresser, Laura S.; Tamura, Anna H. *Archeology at the Gate: Archeological Investigations at the Entrance to Minidoka Relocation Center.* National Park Service, Western Archeological and Conservation Center. 2003. Tamura, Anna. "Gardens below the Watchtower: Gardens and Meaning in World War II Japanese Americans Incarceration Camp," *Landscape Journal* 23.1 (2004), 1–21. National Park Service. *Cultural Landscapes Inventory: Minidoka Internment National Monument.* 2007. Tamura, Anna. "Minidoka Gardens." In Tremayne, Russell and Todd Shallot, eds. *Surviving Minidoka: The Legacy of WWII Japanese American Incarceration.* *Boise*: Boise State University College of Social Sciences and Public Affairs, 2013.

FACING Kiyo Kubota, daughter-in-law to Fujitarō, with son Kay at Minidoka.

クボタ ガーデン

Fallow Years

Jamie Ford

KUBOTA GARDEN smiled the way gardens do, in vibrant colors, in shapes both wild and curated, in flowers, shrubs, and fronds unfurling, gravity nudging, until she was kissing the surface of reflecting pools on warm summer afternoons.

Her Japanese maples greeted today's visitors, waving her leaves like hands in a breeze that smelled of evergreen and sweetbox. With a touch of something else, the redolence of sweat from the brows of the Kubota family who had dutifully taken care of her, now twenty acres, since 1927. In response to that care, the Garden bloomed her gratitude, always. Because, like Michelangelo, who once spoke about his most famous statue, "You just chip away the stone that doesn't look like David." In a similar fashion, the patriarch of the family, Fujitarō Kubota, bought a logged-off piece of riparian land that no one wanted and chipped away at the thick brush, the weeds, the deadfall graveyard of trees that fell in a forest unheard. His labors revealed the Garden's natural springs, ponds, and a creek that gurgled and flowed until July, when it ran dry, only to be reborn with the rains of September. Fujitarō diligently cut trails for her, dug ponds, and hauled boulders and rocks from farmers' fields. He coaxed beauty and serenity out of every acre. The Garden—her potential that lay hidden—now beamed with joy in orange marigolds, blue pansies, red madrona, and rich green sage.

Today the Garden was especially happy, because birds were warbling their songs of courtship as a young couple alighted her footpaths in kimonos. The bride in white, the groom in black, equal parts happiness and nervous tension. Always hospitable, the Garden waved her leaves, beckoning the couple toward a quiet spot near a reflecting pool to have their photos taken. She smiled as the joyful pair posed in traditional Shinto wedding garb, which always made her feel special and in communion with Shikoku, the birthplace of Fujitarō, who brought the spirit of Japan's smallest island to America. It was Fujitarō who transported the towering beauty of Mount Ishizuchi, the fertility of the peach orchards of Takamatsu, the cleansing power of the Yoshino River, and the reverence and peace of Shikoku's eighty-eight temples to the Garden.

The Garden was proud to be an extension of that place. An oasis of Zen, in the concrete desert of Seattle, with its noisy trains, overcast skies, and everywhere the fetid aroma of low tide and the itchy smell of burning wood. She was honored to take care of the Kubotas, their friends and family, their neighbors and community.

So as the couple smiled and giggled for the camera, the Garden blew them a kiss of honeysuckle, her fragrance lofted on the breeze, settling in like a midwife who had known them since birth.

Spring 1942

THE GARDEN, LIKE MOST gardens, had a favorite season. The summer was much too short. Autumn was prismatic, but her colors always faded like the memory of a happy, lucid dream. And even though she was still plainly beautiful in the winter months, when the evergreens would proudly live up to their name, seizing the spotlight they'd been waiting for all year, there was nothing quite as magical as springtime.

Springtime was when the rocks would no longer rely on the moss and lichen they'd worn as winter coats. Spring was when the frost had long since vanished and the garden delighted visitors with a blizzard of sakura, pink blossoms on blooming cherry trees that looked like cotton candy, and white flowers that settled like freshly fallen snow. The redbuds; magnolias, jasmine, and mahonia, as magnificent as they were, looked on in quiet jealousy. Spring was when the songbirds would return.

The Garden spread her arms wide as the gates were opened, knowing that spring would also be her busiest season. Homeowners and landscape architects would come for her small trees and saplings, shrubs and grasses. The Garden was happy to share.

Then the locals and tourists would show up to gather flowers to help celebrate tea ceremonies, folk dances, and the annual Spring Matsuri Festival. Busloads of schoolchildren from Beacon Hill would visit her on field trips, touching everything in sight, tickling the Garden to her delight. Later would come the elders with cotton hair seeking to be reborn like perennial flowers. They would arrive with walking canes in wrinkled hands. Stooping like them, her branches would become canopies, giving them shade on sunny days and shelter during rainstorms. Finally, air horns would sound in the distance and blue-collar workers from Japantown would find their way to her on weekends to appreciate her natural beauty, her familiar sights and smells that made them feel less homesick.

As the gates stood open day after day the Garden's trees stood tall as she waited to greet the crowds, the smiling, happy people.

But they never came.

Not to be discouraged, the Garden bloomed and bloomed, with more hope than vanity, wanting to be noticed, yes, but also yearning to fulfill her purpose once again. Because a Garden is nothing without someone to appreciate her.

A few people arrived.

First was the elderly man who came and sat on a stone bench. He opened a lunch box, appearing uninterested in the rice and pickled vegetables within. He stared into the distance and chewed his lip. The Garden spread her branches so the warmth of the sun could find him, but even so, the man sighed wearily. He took off his hat and drew a note from his coat pocket. He unfolded the piece of paper, labeled Executive Order 9066. She watched the man with growing concern as he read the paper and then folded it back up and tucked it away. He looked at his watch, closed his lunch box, and wandered off, disappearing from the Garden's view as she waved goodbye.

There were the couples, too, though not many. Those who came now looked solemn, as though they were attending a funeral, though they now arrived in Western clothing instead of the formal black attire of a Shinto memorial. They walked slowly, as though in mourning. When a young woman scooped up handfuls of sakura blossoms, inhaling their fragrance, the Garden felt hopeful. Then she let them fall, floating away on the surface of a pond as snow geese honked their annoyance. The Garden had been used to hearing these couples laughing, smiling, but now they only whispered. She held her breath and watched as they dabbed at tears that formed in the corners of their eyes as they said, "I can't believe they're taking us away," and "We'll lose everything, but at least we'll be together."

Then the Garden noticed members of the Kubota family. Some looked angry. Some resigned. All of them upset as they argued and consoled each other. They walked through her acreage as she twirled her flowers to try and make them smile. But they didn't notice as they pointed to their favorite spots, the places they'd labored over most. They talked about hopes and dreams that may never come to fruition.

That's when the Garden spotted Fujitarō, alone, tending to the freshly dug basin for what would be a new pond. She watched as her caretaker kept working, relentlessly, methodically, like he always had, trying to improve every square foot, finding the hidden beauty in every square inch. She wanted to reach out to Fujitarō, to ask what was wrong, but the elderly man couldn't hear her whispers. If he had, the man would have heard her leaves rustling, "It's okay if you go. I'll still be here. I'll always be here for you." Instead all he heard was the trickle of water over stone.

Fall 1943

THE GARDEN HAD NEVER truly been alone. Once Fujitarō had brought her to life, he'd been her constant companion. She had enjoyed the company of workers and visitors, friends and family. Her life had been full. But last year she'd watched as Fujitarō closed the iron gates during a spring rainstorm. He'd laced chains around them. Then she heard the heavy click of a padlock. She waved her branches and leaves as he walked away into the mist without a raincoat. She didn't understand why everyone had left. Why did they have to go? Where had they gone? Not just the Kubota family, but everyone—the people who came to buy saplings and flowers, the workers, the couples, the families, the busloads of children. The Garden's questions remained unanswered.

All that remained were the birds. The squirrels.

An occasional black-tailed deer who ate its way through a hedgerow.

They seemed lonely too as the gates had remained shut throughout the summer, the winter, and well into the following year—this year. Now the gates were covered with moss, touches of creeping ivy, and boughs of willow that had fallen in a windstorm. The Garden couldn't imagine spring without the Kubotas. Who would brush away the fragrant pine needles that blanketed the ground? Who would skim the ponds? Who would carefully plant chrysanthemums that would bloom and announce the beginning of a new year? The maples and cedars had grown, unpruned, their leaves uncollected, slowly smothering the grass beneath. The hedges grew wild like uncombed hair, the shrubs gave way to thickets of weeds and thorns, prickles and nettles. Without care from Fujitarō and his family, she felt like an unmade bed. Comfortable, but disorderly, and empty.

Then one day she had visitors.

The Garden stood tall, spread her arms wide. She eagerly watched the people use a tool to snap the lock from the gates. She heard the sound of metal on concrete as the chains fell. The gates groaned when opened, cracking off bits of rust. She smiled as the men wandered in because they had uniforms and helmets that were dull green, that seemed to blend into her grasses and hedges. Perhaps they were workers who'd come to take care of her in Fujitarō's absence. She felt hopeful as they strolled along every path, crossing every footbridge, brushing aside wild branches that were blocking their passage. But they simply walked, occasionally stopping, pointing, as though they were looking for something, or someone. Her branches hung low and her leaves began to fall like tears as she heard one of them say, "See, there's nothing here."

Winter 1944

THE GARDEN FELT COLD. More than cold, abandoned. She'd stood in the rain for months that turned to sleet, and eventually snow, the weight of which snapped many of her lovely magnolia branches. Her fallen oak leaves, pinecones, and needles had been left to rot. She smelled like a lost forest, damp and miserable. What was once beautiful, trimmed, sculpted, meticulously cared for, was now idlewild, weed-infested, pocked by fungus and banana slugs. The birds were gone as well. She felt forgotton again, her ponds and reflecting pools now reflected neglect and despair.

From her treetops, the Garden peered down at Seattle each day, yearning. She looked through the morning fog, toward the horizon, beyond where her people had boarded trains and left. She listened for the rumble of delivery trucks. Occasionally getting her hopes up that they might stop, that the passengers would pay her a visit, but they always drove past. Eventually she gave up hoping.

By night she saw a city on guard, airplane factories to the south, nearly invisible, hidden by camouflage. Cars with blue running lights. Homes with blackout curtains, and the occasional warship at dock. Once a month she'd be awakened by sirens, horns wailing, as searchlights lit up the cloudy night sky.

Each month that passed, she wondered about the Kubotas. Each month she wondered if they were ever coming back.

During these dark and fallow years, the Garden's loneliness had only been interrupted a handful of times, and always by boys from Franklin High School, who snuck in on Friday and Saturday nights. They smelled like aftershave, wore lettermen's jackets, brought flashlights and cans of Olympia beer that they drank, crushed, and left behind in their wake of restlessness and churning hormones.

As noisy and unpleasant as they were, the Garden longed for companionship. Anyone was better than no one, she told herself, so she always tried to shelter the boys from the weather, blocking the wind with her trees and remaining leaves, as they smoked cigarette after cigarette and told stories to one another. The Garden didn't like the smell of burning tobacco, so she held her breath as long as she could.

Tonight, the boys were quieter than normal. "This is for all the kids who aren't graduating with us." A boy with a crewcut said, holding up his beer. "I don't care what some people say, they were our classmates and they should at least be allowed to come home and finish the year. Besides, our baseball team just isn't the same."

"Here's to 'em," another boy said as he jumped up and wiped wet leaves from the backside of his jeans, "Gone but not forgotten." The boy finished his can of beer and threw it over the trees. Two other boys chugged their cans and threw them as well.

The Garden felt the cans bounce off. She heard the pinging of tin as they found their way to the ground. She sighed, exhaling, as her cool breath whipped up leaves and pine needles, and snuffed out the boys' cigarettes. She didn't mean to. She wanted to quietly listen to what they had to say. Despite their rough behavior, she felt their kindness as well. But the boys took the wind as their cue and left anyway.

Fall 1945

AS WINTER ENDED, the Garden might have worried about a killer frost, when the temperature reached the dew point and everything is covered in thin layers of ice, but the weather didn't matter anymore. No one had planted anything for three years.

Though she did feel better in the spring, because at least the sparrows returned, the geraniums and begonia that remained somehow found room to grow among the weeds, and the cherry trees, though gangly and untrimmed, once again made their presence felt as one-hundred thousand pink blossoms radiated hope and life and vitality. The fragrance from the blooming sakura met the stench from the standing water in the ponds that had gone untended for too long. The two scents fought for attention as the Garden tried not to take sides. (She was rooting for the sakura, of course).

By fall she was dropping seedlings and acorns in earnest, hoping wild growth would be better than no growth. The Garden had promised that she'd always be here for the Kubotas. That she'd remain, patiently waiting for them, in this lifetime or the next. They had given her breath and in return, she would keep breathing. But she hadn't seen them in more seasons than she could remember.

That's when she heard the gates open. The groaning of metal on metal as the rust on iron hinges gave way. She looked up and saw a familiar man. He wore a suit and tie. The man removed his hat and the Garden dropped red and orange maple leaves as though they were tears of joy. But the look on his face told her that she was much happier to see him than he was to see her, regarding the derelict condition that had befallen her. The Garden watched as Fujitarō walked the overgrown paths that he'd once carved by hand, which were now covered in weeds. He knelt down and touched the surface of a reflecting pool that had become filled with silt and debris. He looked up at her pine and yew, her birch and cypress that had endured. She watched as the man walked to an old shed and disappeared inside. She worried that the man might return with herbicides and poisons. That it was too much effort to pull the weeds from the flowers. Too hard to rein in the wild growth that had nearly swallowed the Garden whole. Much easier to kill it all, cut the trees down, put her out of her misery and begin again. But the man emerged with a simple, dusty rake. She watched as he fought his way through weeds and bushes until he reached the place where he'd once dug a pond as he and his family were about to be taken away. She looked on as he removed his jacket and hung it on one of her branches.

He touched the bark of one of her red maples, patting the old tree and said, "I know you can't hear me, but it's okay. I'm still here. I'll always come back for you."

The Garden smiled once again.

Then the man loosened his tie, rolled up his sleeves, and got to work.

The Garden Reconsidered

Glenn Nelson

I HAVE ONE FAMILY PORTRAIT from my childhood. It is black and white because, well, *that* past had no pigmentation except in our own misty, water-colored memories. These days I gaze upon that snapshot with different eyes. They see this picture more hypothetically now. My mother is so young and beautiful—and so hopeful looking, holding my baby sister while my brother and I squint into the sun. We're all definitely of Japanese stock, at least the one-sixteenth that would have targeted us, along with some 120,000 American Japanese, for forcible removal. Two-thirds of those taken were U.S. citizens, like us. The triggering decree, Executive Order 9066, was signed by a U.S. president, Franklin D. Roosevelt.

If my family portrait had been taken a few years earlier, we and whatever of our lives' possessions we could carry in our arms might have been dragged off to a holding area in some animal stall at the state fairgrounds. We might have been stamped as "alien enemies," emphasizing our otherness as if we swooped into this sweet land of liberty on saucers. Our next stop might have been the middle of nowhere, behind barbed wire, in Idaho, like most families of Japanese ancestry who were uprooted from the Seattle area.

But none of that ever happened to us. My mother is from Niigata in the north of the main island of Honshu, where she was during the war. I was born in Tokyo. We moved almost immediately to Seattle, where my father worked at Boeing and my mother raised her three children. That meant that Japanese culture subsumed our household. We flew carp windsocks on Boys' Day and Girls' Day. We danced at the *obon* festival. We sometimes ate fish for breakfast. I rolled sushi for my fourth-grade class. I went to Japan twice and during one of those trips met the Japanese Babe Ruth, Sadaharu Oh. I knew and saw and tasted things about which Americans twice my half-Japaneseness were ignorant. My mother's family was in the camera business in Japan. My uncle won an Emperor's Award for photography. I got good grades and went to an Ivy League graduate school. When I covered the Olympic Games in Seoul, the South Koreans, as I had feared, instantly recognized the Japanese in me. *I came to America on a boat*, for goshsakes.

I often felt superiorly Japanese to those who were full-blooded but not first-generation. I looked at myself as being Japanese who also was American, not necessarily Japanese American. The U.S. was the place I lived, not the arbiter of my identity, except in one regard: The incarceration story always loomed as some kind of cultural litmus test and therefore a barrier for me to the Japanese American community. As such, the authenticity of my Japanese roots produced a lens through which I saw certain parts of my world, including Kubota Garden. It always felt representative of my experience and was accessible because it was located in southeast Seattle, where I grew up and still live. It massaged my Japanese soul. The flow and vibe felt familiar. I now realize that I focused on the waterfalls, streams and ponds, wooden bridges, rocks, lanterns, and maple trees because they were expected and echoed the beauty I beheld with families and friends during my visits to my birthplace. The garden went through a period of neglect about the time I was attending college, but I don't really remember it appearing unkempt because all I saw was its Japanese-ness. For me, those elements never faded.

As with my family portrait, my vision of Kubota Garden began to change in 2017. I chose that year, which marked seventy-five since the World War II concentration camps were introduced and sixty since my birth, to visit concentration camp sites starting with Minidoka. That's where Fujitarō Kubota was incarcerated. Yes, *that* Kubota. When I arrived outside Twin Falls, Idaho, for the opening picnic of the Minidoka Pilgrimage, I'd never seen such an assemblage of Americans of Japanese descent. Their being largely strangers, I felt a deeply sad realization that I didn't really know a lot of Japanese Americans. My mother's friends usually were expatriates like her. If we knew any camp survivors, we might not have been aware because they weren't talking about their experiences. When I told my mother that I was visiting the camps, she shrugged and said, "I don't know anything about that." I consequently felt a certain detachment at the pilgrimages, in

addition to a tinge of envy, as if I were attending someone else's class reunion. These were people connected by a deep experience, albeit a horrific one. They greeted each other with hearty hugs. They knew each other's families and had life events on which to catch up. I watched all of this from the outside.

I learned of my mother's wartime experiences only recently, in preparation for writing this chapter. She was in Japan during the worldwide conflict. Her father was in the Japanese military and died during World War II, though not as a kamikaze pilot as I'd bizarrely imagined for much of my life. He succumbed to an illness he'd probably contracted in some faraway jungle. My mother visited him in the infirmary on the way to school. One day, he was gone. One day, so was the family house, burned to the ground. The town rallied to build her family a new one, but it was small, and my grandmother was a single parent with five children. My mother was farmed out to her grandparents, who treated her harshly. They were fairly prosperous fruit growers who taught my mother to hate, to this day, much of their bounty. They'd forbidden her to eat anything but the half-rotten, insect-infested pieces she could find on the ground.

During my pilgrimage to Minidoka, I found myself in a big auditorium full of my own people—mixed-race Japanese, every one. It was like being blind my whole life, blinking my eyes open, and suddenly being able to see myself. At Minidoka, I also attended what was called an intergenerational session. Each group was randomly composed of a survivor of Minidoka, young people, middle-aged people, and older people. We were to share our experiences with the incarceration. I'd thought about passing, out of respect. My past didn't seem to reside on the same emotional plane. Steve, a guy I met earlier, went early. He was kind of a smart aleck, and I'd figured him for someone whose emotions were tied in a knot inside and whose humor was used to conceal that fact. He talked about his father and uncle, a couple of so-called "no-no boys." That meant they answered no to the last two questions, Nos. 27 and 28, on a "loyalty questionnaire" administered by the War Relocation Authority. No. 27 asked if Nissei men would serve on combat duty wherever ordered; No. 28 asked for unqualified allegiance to the U.S. and forsworn allegiance of any form to the Emperor of Japan. Steve, the erstwhile tough guy, melted down during his telling.

Sobbing quietly with the rest of them, I realized that it was the horror and heartbreak of war, and the love and heroism required to overcome it, that aligned all of us.

That experience binds us, but it also defines our American experience. Japanese immigrants and their descendants have been conferred with a special level of otherness in U.S. history. We have been feared, barred, subdued, exiled, mocked, celebrated, and even emulated. This country

seems to keep changing its mind about us, so we have contributed to our own marginalization, chasing the American dream in the shadows, the better to avoid being the nail from the Japanese proverb that gets hammered down. Even the "model minority" myth is an unwanted tribute because it is accompanied by a target. You will hear many concentration-camp survivors say they didn't talk about their experiences because they feared it could happen again. Decades later, they seem prescient.

You cannot listen to the most intimate details of people's lives and offer nothing in return. Some of what emerged during the intergenerational discussion had been repressed for seventy-five years, after all. So I decided to speak to the gathering. I told them how my father, a white guy from a part of Washington state known for its wheat, fell in love with my mother, a young beauty from a part of Japan renowned for its rice. My father had written to his mother about his engagement to this Japanese woman. Instead of writing back, she telegraphed my father's commanding officer. My father was re-stationed for seven months at a place called Sado Island and ordered to "think things over." I later learned that Sado Island is so isolated, throughout Japanese history it is where the vanquished were exiled.

When I finished my story, the survivor in our group looked up, touched my hand, and softly said, "You are like the rest of us."

That moment fitted me with a new lens through which I now view Kubota Garden. Though thoroughly familiar, it is a place I've never completely and truly seen. I finally have noticed the trees and shrubs and even artwork that are native to our region and not purely Japanese. I find the energy of the place to be more embracing, and less precious, pristine, and unapproachable than Japanese gardens I've visited in Seattle and elsewhere in the world.

Kubota Garden, I realize, is a true reflection of its creator, a man from Japan who evolved into Japanese American, with Minidoka playing a critical role in the transformation. It speaks to the entirety of me because it also is my experience. Now I understand that I had to go to Minidoka, a place I'd never been, to find myself and the true essence of Kubota Garden, a place I've visited for most of my life.

追放

Terra Firma

We walked mother, daughter
through iron gate into verdant womb
sensing all paths were equally right
we would not see each other for a while
wanted to spend time together
do things mothers and daughters do.

We climbed the flank of a mountain
forest landscape embracing us early morning
and with each skyward step
whatever easy words we had been speaking
fell off from us
like ripened leaves break off their branches,
but to tell the truth, words had long before
fallen from our trees.

From the mountain top
thirty five years of exile spread below us
decades of struggling alone
with our hearts of darkness
war years never spoken of
the grind of living life
for years at the margins
keeping fears inside so as
not to worry the other.

We were warriors each of us

though we did not know it

the silence we came to understand

as normal corroded the wood of us,

wounded us to ourselves and to each other.

The morning wore on leaf upon leaf,

bark on bark. Side by side sitting on a bench

we ate our picnic lunch

I chewed and listened to the waterfall nearby

the silence of my mother

is the silence of her own mother

and my silence is that of all the mothers

and grandmothers before us, it said.

Generations of women who learned to do,

rather than speak, to survive.

What patient gardeners

each of my female ancestors must have been

pruning and clipping away parts of themselves

to let their young ones grow tall, become trees.

Maple against spruce, ginkgo against cedar

emerald lawns, mossy moss, celluloid harmony

plus friendly carp on spring fed pond

conspiracy of garden revealing

my mother's quiet, inner partiture.

Words fail, they often do,

but on this day of leaf bark stone

what was left unsaid spun terra firma

gurgle and froth of waterfall's song told me so.

CLAUDIA CASTRO LUNA

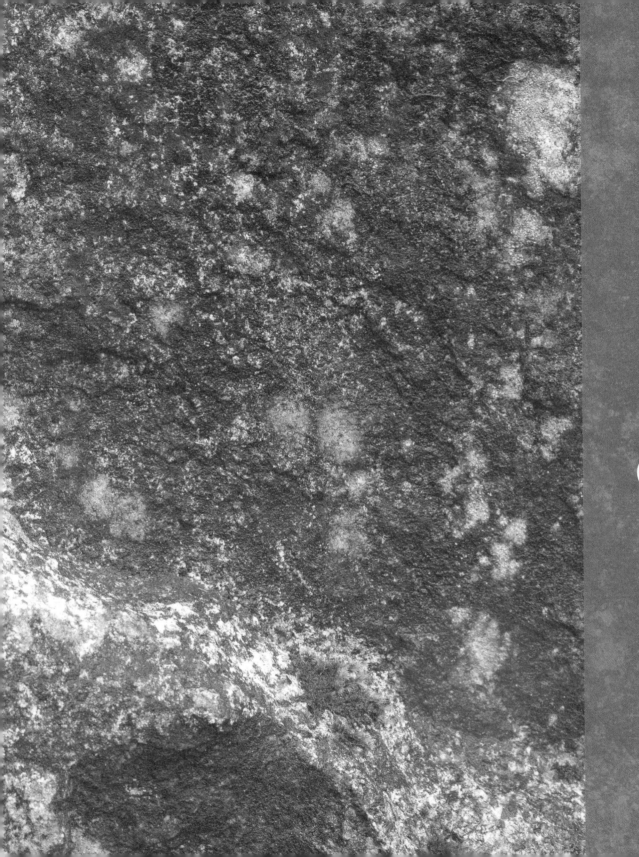

成長
growth

A Private Notion

Iain Robertson

I have evolved a private notion about the importance of landscape,
 and I willingly admit to seeing "characters" almost as functions of a landscape.
LAWRENCE DURRELL

BLUFF BEIGE WALLS HINT: herein is somewhere different.

Lively gates promise intrigue.

A patch of lawn invites sitting but paths, narrow and wide, beckon.

A family of rocks says "hello" while a bell's tongue is still.

A weeping fir gangles atop a deep laurel hedge framing a view.

Even on tiptoes this window tantalizingly conceals more than it reveals,
offering only hints of the delights that lie ahead. The stage is set for
exploration in the valley below but you can't get there from here.

A path nudges us off in a different direction.

So begin the cat-and-mouse games of concealing and revealing that
are part of Kubota Garden's charm and confusion.

We are about to be entranced and embraced, immersed and released,
lost and found in Kubota Garden.

"For a man needs only to be turned round once with his eyes shut in this world to be lost,"
says Thoreau, we turn the first corner, open-eyed, and are lost in the garden's delights. Vanilla
Seattle melts into Kubota Garden's magical embrace. Bland urbanity becomes texture and nuance.
Jostling and nudging shrubs bulge in upon us. Jaded senses awaken. "To return to our sense is to
renew our bond with this wider life, to feel the soil beneath the pavement, to sense—even when
indoors—the moon's gaze upon the roof."[1] No more bland pavement, the ground beneath our feet
is gritty and rutted. We feel.

Turning another corner, we become explorers, lost in the great unknown, consumed by
varied greens, enveloped by a magical world. "Only as we come close to our senses, and begin
to trust, once again, the nuanced intelligence of our sensing bodies, do we begin to notice and
respond to the subtle logos of the land."[2]

What does the land whisper as we walk Kubota Garden's braided paths (a tessellation
disrupted by the land's bucking and buckling)? Following one narrow thread after another bodily
senses and minds become interwoven into the garden's fabric.

We encounter delights: the great terraced overlook, a pond seemingly perched on the hillside,
a low retaining wall of rounded boulders chinked with finer stones. "All senses give us a world, but
the visual one has the greatest definition and scope. This expansive visual world is both sensual
and intellectual. It is sensual, not only because of its colors and shapes, but also because of its
tactile quality."[3] We find ourselves lost in the magic of novelty and intrigue.

The overlook keeps the garden at arm's length, but rounded stepping stones, set steeply into
the hillside, invite us to slip from the terrace's vastness back into a tactile embrace, for to be at
Kubota Garden is to be intimately in it, its compressions and releases among its ponds and places,
its rocks and ravine but most of all among its plants for it is the trees and shrubs, in all their variety
of textures, colors, sizes, and forms that are the heart of the garden's experience. "Open our eyes,

and the world spreads before us in all its vividness and color; close them, and it is instantly wiped out and we are plunged into darkness. One moment, the world is an enticing space inviting us to enter; the next, it' collapses to the limit of our body and we are helplessly disoriented."[4] As they nudge and jostle us on the narrow trails, the plants open our eyes and minds to the here and now of where we are—Kubota Garden.

The garden's experiences are vivid in wide-eyed ways. Trails creep through bulging shrub masses; they pass alongside and through hedges and do so in ways that unsettle our sense of direction. Soon, so soon, we don't know where we are but, no matter, anticipation of what may lie around the bend consumes our attention. Intrigue draws us on. We push along narrow paths through shrub masses waist-high, chest-high, above our heads—a visual as well as physical embrace. Breaking out into the open we find ourselves lost on convoluted lawns of surprise bays and protruding plant promontories. Unceasing variety draws us on. Intricacy upon intricacy unfolds. Layer upon varied layer enriches. Still pools delight. Enchanting bridges invite. Rills and falls draw us, by convoluted paths, up and up the steep hillside to a world-encompassing view. Quotidian reality shrivels. A new meridian supervenes.

Sensory surfeit stirs perceptual alertness. Intimacy attunes more careful attention than we usually accord the world around us. Lost in the garden, we are taken out of ourselves. Sensory experience gives place to speculation: Who? What? How? How did this incongruous variety of forms, this textural surfeit, this mongrel diversity, this weeping and contorted extravagance come about? How did these uncanny rows of large, close-spaced trees come about? From where does this spirit of lively playfulness, unfettered extravagance, and freedom unconstrained by convention come? What is the source of this unusual personality? When the mind takes over from the senses we think differently. "Somehow to see is to think and to understand: sight is coupled with insight, and to exercise the mind is to see with 'the mind's eye.'"[5] What is the hand and mind behind all this beauty? Someone must have conceived the idea lightly and wielded the heavy shovel. Someone drew inspiration from this place while reconstructing a memory from elsewhere.

"As a poet of the historic consciousness, I suppose I am bound to see landscape as a field dominated by the human wish—tortured into farms and hamlets, ploughed into cities. A landscape scribbled with the signatures of men and epochs. Now, however, I am beginning to believe that the wish is inherited from the site; that man depends for the furniture of his will upon his location in space, tenant of fruitful acres or a perverted wood. It is not the impact of his free will upon nature which I see (as I thought) but the irresistible growth, through him, of nature's own blind specified doctrines of variation. She has chosen this poor forked thing as an exemplar."[6]

Do we discern that paths were roads along which Model T Fords trundled, tree rows were a nursery from which plants were plucked to grace gardens around the city, the great hillside and pond necklace were display gardens? Do we comprehend the hints that all was busy, changing, and dynamic, until the curtain fell?

"Our human landscape is our unwitting autobiography reflecting our tastes, our values, our aspirations, and even our fears, in tangible, visible form. We rarely think of landscape that way, and so the cultural record we have 'written' in the landscape is liable to be more truthful than most autobiographies because we are less self-conscious about how we describe ourselves."[7]

The curtain fell but the plants, possessing no notion of human tragedy, continued to grow, as they do now, responsive only to the day's sunlight, the seasons' dictates. Human plays are arrested but nature's play continues unabated.

The garden whispers all around us. It is a mirror of which we are a face. Herein lies its charm, its poignancy, its tragedy. Herein lies its perpetuation or potential downfall.

A mirror of life, life Kubota Garden balances uneasily on the knife-edge of human intention and chance. *Ars est longa, vita brevis.* As we read the garden's story more deeply in its rutted paths and half-overwhelmed rocks, as we become more attentive to its florid spring extravaganzas, so we discern the interplay of human intention and chance, so we feel inklings of human aspirations interacting with plant growth—the shuffle of chance, the cards that have been dealt, the hand that has been played. Imagining ourselves in total control of our destinies, we uneasily discern chance playing a larger hand in our lives than we like to admit. We intuit the waves of events that may overwhelm or sweep forward our fortunes. We may experience the surprise of unanticipated outcomes.

"It is proper and important to think of cultural landscape as nearly everything that we can see when we go outdoors. The basic principle is this: that all human landscape has cultural meaning, no matter how ordinary that landscape may be."[8]

Fortune's twists and turns generate perpetual surprise. As we traverse these magical spaces and experiences, we have an inkling that our delights are the result of hard work thwarted by implacable forces. Kubota Garden is a paradoxical place in which innocent delight surmounts squalid irony. It plays, with passion, the hand it has been dealt. And having taken with one hand, with her other hand fortune has favored the garden with a sustaining gardener—for garden is more real as a verb than a noun, and so it continued, learning, year by year, more about itself and its place. We are not entirely at the mercy of circumstances; our actions can influence our lives and futures—a garden is to garden. But we teeter, as I said, upon a knife-edge.

Development and noise crowd the garden's margins but, more pertinently and pervasively, the plants continue to grow, and grow, and grow. Year by year, decade by decade, the garden transforms itself, perpetually threatening to become an overgrown biography.

In places we sense the shadow of sublime terribilita: plants that are distorted, disfigured and dying as a result of intense competition for space and light. In places overgrown gloom overwhelms "in Stygian Cave forlorn/'Mongst horrid shapes, and shrieks, and sights unholy."[9] But round every dark corner Kubota Garden offers vistas of lightness and unexpected charms. Particularly in spring. Particularly in fall. Particularly in summer and winter. This is a place where the push and pull between nature's growth and human control is palpable. But although on the cusp of ruin, human effort and love have preserved the garden from being overwhelmed by nature's exuberance. Kubota Garden's current glory teeters on dissolution. The knife-edge cuts both ways— control or chaos. Its presence is its history. Its past and present make it unique. in an era where places and experiences are interchangeable, Kubota Garden is its distinct unselfconscious unpretentious self rather than something or somewhere else or, worse still, nowhere at all. We sense this the moment we pass its gate and the more lost we become in its intricacies, the more we are entangled in its web of experiences, the more we find ourselves. "The mind thinks it knows its way around the heart."[10]

How do we honor and preserve Kubota Garden's unpretentious enthusiasm? How can we preserve the identity of this place whose magic invites us to step outside ourselves, our place, and our times? Let's not sanitize, regularize, conventionalize, or normalize it. Visit Kubota Garden and fall under its spell.

Endnotes

1 Abrams, David (1996) *The Spell of the Sensuous* (Pantheon).

2 Ibid, 268.

3 Tuan, Yi-Fu.

4 Ibid.

5 Ibid.

6 Durrell, Lawrence (1957) *Justine*. Alexandria Quartet #1 (E.P. Dutton).

7 Lewis, Pierce F., (1979) "Axioms for Reading the Landscape. Some Guides to the American Scene," in *The Interpretation of Ordinary Landscapes. Geographical Essays* (Oxford University Press).

8 Ibid.

9 Milton, John, "L'Allegro."

10 Ferlinghetti, Lawrence (2005) *Americus 1* (New Directions).

成長

Forgive me,
Mr. Kubota,

for napping
beside your *Rosa rugosa*, underneath
this lush *Omato* maple.
For letting the susurrating poplars
shush me to sleep.   I lay down
on the low rock wall and your garden
claimed me. I stopped thinking
about the broken places
on the bridge between *emigrant*
and *immigrant* and how I don't know
how to mend them.

          Dear Mr. Kubota,
I am writing you from a future I fear
would disappoint you, despite
the way your conifers define
this neighborhood's skyline
just as I imagine you imagined they would.

I slow-walk your paths. Pause
to watch a water-strider leave undisturbed
the surface of your pond. Koi
gather at the edge, as if returning
the greetings offered: *Buenas tardes.*
Xiàwǔ hǎo. Galab wanaagsan.

But one burnt-orange branch hangs
in a mature pine like a warning lamp
I can't not see.

        Dear Mr. Kubota.
What you made by hand endures
for now. The springs you shaped into streams,
the cast-off stones you stretched across them—

ELIZABETH AUSTEN

Still Working

Betsy Anderson

ON A HOT JULY AFTERNOON, visitors to Kubota Garden are greeted by the unusual silhouettes of butoh dancers, perched atop the bridges and among the pines of the Japanese garden. The dancers curl and then unfurl their limbs at a rate only slightly perceptible against the landscape behind them, whose own boughs shift languidly in the thick air. Known as "the dance of darkness," butoh is a postwar form of Japanese dance theater that reveals the close relationship between vulnerability and resilience. It is an apt artistic expression to find within Kubota Garden, which is arguably the most unlikely landscape in the city of Seattle.

That this landscape could be created at all and that it still exists today is cause for wonder. "She is the Just-in-Time garden," observes Mary Anne Parmeter, Rainier Beach community member and an early board member for the Kubota Garden Foundation. In its ninety-two-year history, Kubota Garden has survived racist alien land laws, the Great Depression, the World War II Japanese American incarceration, the automobile, accelerating development pressure, vandalism, and economic change. Throughout, the garden has absorbed and reformed itself around the vicissitudes of American society. The singular resilience and responsiveness of this landscape contribute to its significance as a "Third Place," a term created by sociologist Ray Oldenburg to describe the informal public gathering spaces that are critical to a healthy democratic society.[1]

Fujitarō Kubota and his descendants understood this concept intuitively, long before it was articulated in books, university classrooms, and city planning offices. There, the prevailing academic and professional discourse of the past few decades has emphasized the need to safeguard and rejuvenate the public realm by protecting vestigial "sacred" community spaces or retrofitting isolated suburbs whose development left them out.[2] Oldenburg's Third Place thesis argues that everyone needs an inclusive, accessible place outside the home (the first place) and work (the second place), where they can feel a sense of belonging and agency in shaping their environment.

Over many years, Fujitarō Kubota laid the groundwork for a landscape that would become the democratic heart of Rainier Beach and a primary touchstone for Seattle immigrant communities. The garden's unusual success as a public space hinges on its receptive, vernacular, and spontaneous qualities. These are notoriously difficult conditions to maintain in a landscape that has evolved from the very personal experiment of one family to a city-owned garden, managed by a carefully orchestrated public-private partnership. The garden has achieved this delicate balance for almost a century thanks to a rare succession of sympathetic gardeners, stretching from Fujitarō Kubota's creation of the garden beginning in 1927, through his son Tom Kubota's inheritance of the landscape, to Tom's longtime mentorship of Seattle Parks and Recreation head gardener Don Brooks, who retired in 2018.

It would be a mistake to reduce the garden solely to the product of a single gardener or to a landscape forged only by chance or to a place shaped exclusively by the community. Rather, the garden's vitality as a multicultural public space relies on the dynamic tension between the individual, the community, and natural systems. To date, the succession of Kubota-trained gardeners has built and consistently maintained a framework that is flexible and allows space for the environment to change and for the community to claim the garden as its own. However, the individual agency that makes this flexibility possible is easily threatened by the well-meaning scaffold of policies, bureaucratic structures, and best practices that comprise professional public land management. The garden's historic management style is further imperiled by widespread socioeconomic changes that make another thirty-year tenure like Brooks' seem improbable.

Brooks' departure marks an existential turning point in the garden's development that has inspired significant introspection and reflection about its importance, including a new master-planning process and the book in which this essay sits. As the other chapters in this volume attest, Kubota Garden is a complex palimpsest of culture and nature that merits examination

FACING Don Brooks pruning in the garden.

from an almost endless number of perspectives. However, the lifeblood of the garden's continued existence is the fortuitous spontaneity that shaped it in the first place, allowed it to survive, and continues to manifest itself in its identity as a refuge and a gathering place for the community. Preserving this spontaneity is the most critical task facing the Kubota Garden Foundation and Seattle Parks and Recreation as they chart the future of this landscape.

The Receptive Garden

The preservation of spontaneity smacks of oxymoron. It is more useful instead to understand and preserve the *conditions* that allow such change to take place. Compared with other historic landscapes, Kubota Garden has been remarkably adept at receiving and adapting to change— whether cultural, social, or ecological. This responsiveness has allowed the garden to evolve with its shifting surroundings and has preserved its relevance in the hearts and minds of its neighbors.

The garden's receptive character can be traced to its very founding and identity as a working landscape. Fujitarō Kubota envisioned a display garden for his nursery and design business where he could showcase ideas for potential clients. The composition of plantings and stone was always in flux, and even the most venerable specimen pine was not immune from being uprooted and relocated to a well-heeled garden in Windermere, Laurelhurst, or Magnolia. Most gardens and parks are borne of a desire to leave a lasting imprint on the landscape, one that grows and improves steadily over time with the maturation of trees and shrubs and human attachment. By contrast Kubota's garden, as Iain Robertson has observed, was organized around a disturbance regime and was therefore constantly changing in aspect and composition.[3] "They had no hesitation in taking the best plant out of the garden to use on a job," Brooks recalls. "Because it paid the bills. You can always find something else and start over. That attitude really came through to me. One thing you realize: nothing is permanent."

Kubota's comfort with change and his interest in the garden as a process rather than an artifact echoes a characteristically Japanese embrace of transience. This is demonstrated most saliently by the shrine at Ise. Located in Mie Prefecture, on the island of Honshu, Ise is considered Japan's most sacred Shinto shrine. Its buildings, first constructed in the seventh century, are torn down and rebuilt every twenty years in an effort to preserve the sanctuary's eternal qualities. The rebuilding cycle has only been broken once—during the civil war and unrest of the Sengoku, or "warring states" era (c. 1467 – c. 1568).[4]

The breaking of Kubota Garden's disturbance regime occurred twice, under similarly jarring conditions that coincide with the major turning points in its history: the forced incarceration of

FACING Allan Kubota oversees the move of an old Japanese maple specimen to a new home.

the Kubota family during World War II and the acquisition of the garden by Seattle Parks and Recreation in 1987. The latter marked the end of the garden's working life. As Don Brooks recalls, one of his first tasks as the new head gardener was to go around filling dozens of holes from plants previously removed.

Brooks knew he couldn't replicate the upheaval of the nursery-display era and instead attempted to foster the garden's innate tendency for stand replacement as its large number of sizable trees aged or were felled by storms. Volunteer Douglas-fir had grown up in the garden in the fourteen years since Fujitarō Kubota's death, and Brooks removed them quietly without his supervisor's permission. He was also comfortable augmenting the garden's restrained plant palette with additional species and cultivars, such as new varieties of Japanese maples that seemed in keeping with the Kubota family spirit but appealed to the garden's ever-increasing number of visitors.[5] The freedom that Brooks experienced in making such substantial revisions to the garden would likely be frowned upon by most landscape preservation practitioners. However, this flexibility and its support from the city and the foundation was critical to offset a very strong tendency of the garden to feel frozen in time.

The role of landscape as a witness to change is one of its most significant functions, never more so than in Kubota Garden. Here, the family's hardship and resilience manifests in the fabric of the garden itself, which changed forever as a result of their forced removal from Seattle in 1942 and incarceration at Minidoka Relocation Center in Idaho. Fujitarō Kubota is said to have cried for hours when he returned in late 1945 to find his composition of plantings and ponds choked with weeds and silt. Nursery plantings left in their holding areas for years had gone on with their business of growing, inadvertently creating some of the most distinctive areas in the garden today, including the Dancing Pines and the Contorted Filberts.

The period of neglect fundamentally altered the garden's character, distinguishing it from other Japanese-style gardens in North America and in some ways uniting it more strongly with the Japanese garden tradition. Thomas M. Robinson, whose 1992 master's thesis on Kubota's gardens has become a seminal work, notes that "during the years of neglect… the garden began to develop a new and unique personality through the synthesis of natural processes merging with designed garden areas and nursery stock." He adds, "This process of 'design by chance,' or 'serendipity' created another historical link between Kubota Garden and its traditional predecessors in Japan," noting that the best example of a serendipitous Japanese garden may be Saihoji, "the Moss Temple, [whose] exquisite blankets of moss… established themselves during long periods of neglect that occurred during the Ōnin wars."[6]

Kubota Garden is likewise inscribed with the large movements of history, but it tells a very local story of one family's strength and resolve in the face of injustice. The garden's celebrated scrappy character can be dated to this period; many admirers have described it as having been painted with broad brush strokes. The hardy, almost boisterous quality of Fujitarō Kubota's tenacious and contrasting plant palette—so at odds with the traditional Japanese garden imagined by most Americans—nonetheless seems to invite more public engagement with the garden than would happen within a highly manicured landscape. "It's not fussy," explains Mary Anne Parmeter. "There has to be kind of an ad hoc quality to it, because that's part of the magic. It has a certain crudity to it, but it has a heck of a lot of energy in it. That's what is lovely."

The Vernacular Garden

Scholars of Third Places and community sacred spaces, such as Ray Oldenburg and Randy Hester, tout the humble, homely nature of these venues. A "low profile," as Oldenburg calls it, is critical to a successful Third Place because it discourages self-consciousness among those who gather there and ensures that the space is valued for its substance rather than its appearance.[7] While there is a key distinction to make between a highly polished, corporate environment and the Third Place, reducing the comparison to one of ostentation versus humility overlooks the critical role of the individual space creator.

We do not have a great word to describe a place that retains the indelible ethos of its author while still allowing—and this is crucial—space for others. *Vernacular* may be the closest we can get. In a brief essay, writer and cultural geographer J. B. Jackson notes that although the concept has been malleable, "current definitions of the word usually suggest that the vernacular dwelling is designed by a craftsman, not an architect, that it is built with local techniques, local materials, and with the local environment in mind."[8] The Cultural Landscape Foundation defines vernacular landscapes as places "that evolved through use by the people whose activities or occupancy shaped those landscapes... [and that] reflect the physical, biological, and cultural character of those everyday lives."[9]

While Fujitarō Kubota's twenty-acre garden could not be described as a humble project, it is an excellent example of a Pacific Northwest vernacular landscape. Its strength and its popularity derive from the qualities described above and from what historian Marc Treib calls "the unselfconsciousness, the appropriate sense of the makeshift, and the accepted transience of vernacular building."[10] It was a garden built in many ways for the excluded, by the excluded, using the only techniques and materials that were available.

Even though it was primarily a working landscape, a portion of Kubota's nursery, home, and display garden was preserved for public use. Over time the landscape became a cherished community gathering place, made more significant because many who gathered there were not welcome in other places in the city. As Jeff Hou observes, garden spaces like Kubota's provided a rare venue for the Japanese community to host events in an era of racial discrimination. Kubota opened the garden to everyone, however, which cultivated a broad base of support in Rainier Beach for the family and landscape that likely helped both survive World War II and the threat of condominium development.[11]

In addition to the enduring discrimination he faced in Seattle, Kubota was also an outsider to traditional Japanese landscape design. Raised on Shikoku in an agricultural family, Kubota could not formally access the techniques or philosophy cultivated by elite gardeners over generations. "Fujitarō went to Japan, and the Japanese gardeners there wouldn't share a thing with him," recounts Brooks. "It was a closed craft, especially before the war. He got no explanation of things; he had to figure it out by himself."

Brooks argues that Kubota's can-do approach propelled some of the garden's biggest projects, including the Mountainside, and that the family was never deterred by a lack of technical expertise or financial resources. When Seattle Parks and Recreation staff replaced the roof of the Mountainside shelter, Brooks urged them to preserve the same materials and homespun construction techniques: "There were joist hangers, there was plywood, there were nails sticking through—perfect. That was the work that the Kubotas did. Tom told me several times, 'We didn't know how to do this, we didn't know how to do that. We just did it.'"

The utilitarian bent of the Kubota family even inscribed itself in the garden's plant material, notably in its signature pines. When Brooks first arrived in the garden, he noticed that a lot of its carefully pruned pines had been neglected as the family's maintenance resources dwindled. The trees' natural growth patterns superseded the pruned forms, resulting in strange projections of growth. "I just had to cut those off and start over," Brooks says. "If you're looking hard at the trees, you can see these awkward ninety- or forty-five-degree angles that are not acceptable in a really well-done tree. I call that the Kubota Angle."

The garden also thumbed its nose at traditional Japanese garden design through its willingness to embrace its changing cultural context. It was not, for example, too precious to welcome the automobile. To allow potential customers to view the display garden in comfort, Kubota installed a system of curving roadways. Thomas Robinson observes that Kubota's "drive-thru Japanese garden" is a unique, twentieth-century American adaptation of an Edo Period

stroll garden: "Winding between masses of trees and shrubs, the road employed the principles of Indirect Approach and Incomplete View in a revolutionary new way... a new mode of access that was appropriate to both the scale of the site and the local culture."[12] To attest to their ongoing relevance, these roadways continued to be used by local youth when the garden first opened to the public in the 1980s.[13]

Fujitarō Kubota's pragmatism and eschewal of elite professionalism was handed down to his son Tom, who taught Don Brooks the family philosophy. As Brooks recalls, this perspective may explain Tom Kubota's skepticism about Robert Murase, the acclaimed landscape architect who was awarded the first master planning contract for the garden in 1990. Brooks remembers Tom complaining that he wanted to walk Murase around the perimeter of the garden, "just walk the outside and look in, and he wasn't interested in that at all."

Murase's vision was recorded on paper, in the plans and written descriptions of a professional landscape architect. This contrasted starkly to the Kubota family approach, which leapt directly from quietly experiencing the site to its hands-on shaping with stone, water, and plants—all done without the intervention of a plan or construction drawings. As is the case for most vernacular landscapes, little to no paper documentation exists for any of the Kubota Gardening Company projects. The historical record that does exist must be gleaned from the physical fabric of extant landscapes, something Brooks became very adept at noticing. "I can still drive around and say— 'the Kubotas built that garden.' You can still see remnants of it by three or four key plants and a stone," he reflects. "They used Japanese maples and some specimen pine, variegated *Pieris*, a bunch of azaleas, and some *Ajuga* groundcover. It's the same stuff that the family uses in their business today."

The People's Garden

When asked why the garden feels so welcoming, Brooks cites Kubota's pervasive aesthetic influence on Pacific Northwest landscapes: "It's welcoming and it's familiar—it's the Seattle landscape. It's what almost everybody has in their yard, but bigger and bolder." Designed to be imagined in vignettes that potential customers could imagine in a front or back yard, Kubota Garden has a residential scale despite its grand size.

The garden was not created for a rich patron, nor was it intentionally built with public funds as a civic space. Despite being created by one family on originally private land, it is an inherently communitarian, eminently accessible place. A series of fortuitous circumstances have rescued the garden in the nick of time and ensured remarkable continuity in its evolution and management.

Significantly, it has—at least to date—been spared the type of manipulation that could easily befall a landscape with more overtly stated intentions.

There is real danger that an effort to preserve the garden and attract more visitors may undermine the very qualities that have allowed it to endure and become a sacred space of south Seattle. This is the challenge that the new master planning process, undertaken by Jones & Jones, must embrace. Without awareness and sensitivity, the garden could be easily scrubbed of the Third Place characteristics that have long nurtured a vibrant, diverse, respectful, and joyous community life. For the garden to survive these efforts to shape her future, she must principally be understood not as an artifact but as a spontaneous system woven of stone, water, plants, and people.

Endnotes

1 Oldenburg, Ray (1989) *The Great Good Place* (De Capo Press).

2 Ibid.

   Hester (2010) *Design for Ecological Democracy* (MIT Press).

3 Robertson, Iain (May 8, 2018) Unpublished notes from Kubota Garden master plan workshop.

4 Coaldrake, William H. (1996) *Architecture and Authority in Japan* (Routledge) 18.

5 Brooks, Don (August 7, 2018) Interviewed by Betsy Anderson.

6 Robinson, Thomas M., (1992) *Traditions in Translation: The Gardens of Fujitaro Kubota.* (Master's thesis, University of Washington) 114.

7 Oldenburg, 36–37.

8 Jackson, John Brinckerhoff (1984)"Vernacular," in *Discovering the Vernacular Landscape*, (Yale University Press) 85.

9 Cultural Landscape Foundation (CLF). "Vernacular Landscapes" https://tclf. org/places/learn-what-are-cultural-landscapes/vernacular-landscapes. Accessed 9 September 2018.

10 Treib, Marc (2002) "Must Landscapes Mean?" in *Theory in Landscape Architecture: A Reader*, edited by Simon Swaffield (University of Pennsylvania Press) 89–108.

11 Hou, Jeffrey (2019) "The Gardens of Arrival," (Chin Music Press) 31.

12 Robinson, 110.

13 Brooks.

成長

Kubota

Yours is the choice
of futures. Survey ravage, see
green. Survey alien, see

home. It doesn't matter
if you live to see it. It doesn't matter
if it never blooms. Just plant

the seed. Mix what you knew
with what you are knowing. Mix
what you were with what

you are becoming. It doesn't matter
if they get your tongue. It doesn't matter
if they kidnap you, fence you in. What's more distance

when you already came so far? There too
you will survey, there too
you will plant. Minidoka, Guantanamo

no match for a seedling. This is your
becoming. You don't know how long
it will last. But what you have cannot be

extinguished. It goes where you go
and it angers them. They do everything
to kill your language. But you know the trees

will speak for you, signing welcome, so you mix
seeds. And someday someone will walk your oasis
more eloquent than any Ellis

Island, under your grand fir more graceful
than any cold cast statue, holding aloft its tuft like a beacon
and they will mouth the names

you so carefully entangled—peony, threadleaf,
kuretake, tanyosho, empress, atlas,
weeping. And feel kin

because they too bear far-
off trees in their blood. And I too
know red dust, bring my gulmohars,

neems and peepals. It doesn't matter
that you never met me. This is my home
you saw. Your future my becoming,

They never could stop your roots.

SHANKAR NARAYAN

Terminology

Our gratitude to Denshō for its help in using the proper language to talk about the mass removal and incarceration of Japanese Americans during World War II. We reprint a sample of their guidance here with their permission.

INCARCERATION VS. INTERNMENT

The commonly used "internment" fails to accurately describe what happened to Japanese Americans during World War II. "Internment" refers to the legally permissible, though morally questionable, detention of "enemy aliens" in time of war. There were approximately eight thousand Issei ("first generation") arrested as enemy aliens and subject to what could be described as "internment" in a separate set of camps run by the Army or Department of Justice. This term becomes a misleading, othering euphemism when applied to American citizens detained by their own government; yet two-thirds of Japanese Americans incarcerated during World War II were U.S. citizens by birth and right.

CONCENTRATION CAMPS VS. RELOCATION CENTERS

FACING Fujitarō Kubota in front of the Japanese Garden at Bloedel Reserve.

There is still some debate over the most appropriate terminology for the camps where Japanese Americans were confined during World War II. At first, Japanese Americans were held in temporary camps the government called "assembly centers"—facilities surrounded by fences and guarded by military police. This term is clearly euphemistic in nature, as the "assembly" was carried out by military and political force. Therefore, we recommend its use only as part of a proper noun (e.g., Puyallup Assembly Center) or in quotation marks for specific references to this type of facility.

Japanese Americans were later transferred to longer-term camps which the government called "relocation centers." (Some officials, including the president, also referred to them as "concentration camps" in internal memos.) Despite the seemingly innocuous name, these were prisons—compounds of barracks surrounded by barbed-wire fences and patrolled by armed guards—which Japanese Americans could not leave without permission. "Relocation center" fails to convey the harsh conditions and forced confinement of these facilities. As prison camps outside the normal criminal justice system, designed to confine civilians for military and political purposes on the basis of race and ethnicity, these sites also fit the definition of "concentration camps."

For more, please go to: *densho.org/terminology*

Keeping the Garden Alive

Joy Okazaki

I GREW UP WITH vivid memories of sneaking into Kubota Garden as a kid, but it never dawned on me that this special place would evolve from a family home, nursery and landscaping business, display and secret garden for generations of Kubota family (and many neighbor kids like me) to a public garden that hundreds of thousands would visit. I'm struck by the number of visitors who've been transformed with an appreciation for nature, Japanese garden design, the resilience and perseverance of the immigrants and citizens of Japanese heritage, and the head-smacking realization that some of the same fears of cultural difference and racial bias that existed when Fujitarō first came to the United States, and were repeated during the years on both sides of World War II, are still prevalent today.

Thanks to strong community voices, the late City Councilmember Jeanette Williams recognized the importance of preserving the legacy of Fujitarō Kubota and his garden. The City of Seattle designated the 4.5-acre core garden as a Historic Landmark in 1981 and eventually purchased the garden in 1987. Since becoming a public park, Kubota Garden has served the community as a rare gathering place, a peaceful sanctuary to walk in nature, take pictures, picnic, attend events, and botanize.

The Kubota Garden Foundation was formed in 1989 with the recognition that Seattle Parks and Recreation did not have the capacity to maintain a historic Japanese garden, and a private nonprofit organization could be an invaluable partner. For the past thirty years, the foundation has carried out its mission to "support, enhance and perpetuate the vision of Fujitarō Kubota and his son Tom Kubota" through the tireless work of volunteers in collaboration with Seattle Parks and Recreation, and through the generous support of donors.

Kubota Garden relies heavily on the partnership of the city and foundation. The foundation has over five hundred members and in 2018 hundreds of volunteers logged nearly eight thousand hours—helping with garden maintenance, guiding tours, holding a spring and fall plant sale, managing the nursery, greeting and surveying visitors, generating publicity, hosting classes and events, and funding projects.

In order to prepare for the next twenty to thirty years, we recently collaborated with Seattle Parks and Recreation and hired Jones & Jones Architects and Landscape Architects and Hoshide Wanzer Architects to create a Master Plan Update that identifies opportunities for garden programming and capital improvements. The key to successfully implementing the master plan is resources. The foundation sees a robust future for the garden, and you can be a part of the legacy. With your support, we can meet the growing needs of the garden.

There are many stories of Grandpa Kubota's perseverance, artistic talent, use of water and stone, and interest in sharing his native Japanese culture and garden design with the people of his adopted country. But what would Fujitarō think about the breadth of the garden's impact? Would he have ever envisioned the garden's future entrusted to uniquely committed city gardeners and an organization of hundreds of volunteers and supporters who preserve the garden and its legacy of an immigrant family that countered oppression with dignity and beauty? How about the recognition from far-flung visitors? Or the garden's value as a place of respite, serenity, and beauty in the colorful urban fabric of the Rainier Beach community? While I'm sure he would be politely embarrassed by the fame, I think he would be quietly pleased that the garden and its spirited stone continues to touch and inspire visitors and readers alike, and will continue to do so for generations to come.

Joy Okazaki
Founding Board Member and current Board President
1989–2019
www.kubotagarden.org

Acknowledgments

Spirited Stone is published with generous support from the Stanley Smith Horticultural Trust; Pendleton and Elisabeth Carey Miller Charitable Foundation; Furthermore: a program of the J. M. Kaplan Fund; David R. Coffin Publication Grant from Foundation for Landscape Studies; 4Culture; and the Robert Chinn Foundation.

We must express our whole-hearted appreciation to the Kubota family for your vision, hard work and sacrifice: Mr. Fujitarō Kubota, your wife Kumae, and your family—Tak and Kiyo, Tom and Amy, May and George Yano. Despite facing injustices, you bestowed upon us a beautiful legacy. Your grandchildren, including Allan, who carries on the business, shared their memories: Allan and Mary Kubota, Linda Kubota Byrd and Marcus Lindstrom, Cathy and Oz Hem, Margo and Jeff Izutsu, Wendy Goade, Michael Yano, and Susan and Michael Mise.

The Kubota Garden Foundation for many years wanted to produce a book about the garden. Somehow another urgent project or program always took precedence. We are grateful to all the past and current Kubota Garden Foundation board members for their unfailing support of the garden through the years. We thank the Foundation's current board members for supporting this project and generously contributing their time, expertise, and funds to its production.

This book would not have been possible without the vision, leadership, and dedication of our publisher Bruce Rutledge of Chin Music Press. When we first met with you to pitch the project, you recognized a story with heart that needed to be told. The authors, poets, photographers, and artists who enthusiastically stepped forward to participate brought the story to life. We are deeply grateful to you, your design team Dan Shafer and Carla Girard, and photographer Gemina Garland-Lewis.

The garden would be just a memory if it were not for the Rainier Beach community and Seattle City Councilmember Jeanette Williams, who in 1987 understood why this landscape was important to protect and found the funding to save it. We are grateful to Seattle Parks and Recreation for taking care of the garden all these years and your close collaboration with the Kubota Garden Foundation. Don Brooks, our first Senior Gardener, worked for more than thirty years to shape this beautiful public space. Since 1927 the garden has had only three senior gardeners—Fujitarō, Tom, and Don. This year Giles Morrish became the fourth Senior Gardener. Along with Marcia High and Amir Williams, he carries on the legacy.

Felicia Gonzalez curated the poetry and helped create a book that reflects the garden's ethos. Your adept way with words helped us find the title and successfully share the spirit of the book in numerous grant applications. Sam and Sally Green of Brooding Heron Press created a beautiful broadside that will support our fundraising campaign. Mary Anne Parmeter, former Foundation board member and historian, architect Johnpaul Jones and landscape architect Duane Dietz of Jones & Jones, Don Brooks, and Southeast Seattle residents Nora Liu, Ron Angeles, Antonia Angeles Hare, and Marcus Harrison Green all made significant contributions. Thank you also to Reverend Robert Giulietti, the Reverend Mitsue Kusuki Giulietti, and associates at the Konkōkyō Church of Seattle.

Ernie Dornfeld, Kubota Garden Foundation Historian, reviewed multiple drafts and offered guidance as we sought to accurately reflect the garden history, write the timeline and find the best archival photographs for publication. Chris Kim, Antonia Angeles Hare, and Joy Okazaki contributed photographs of people in the garden.

Tom Ikeda, Executive Director of Denshō, encouraged our efforts. Thank you to Denshō for hosting a selection of the Kubota Garden Foundation's photo archives in your collection. This was particularly helpful as designers, contributors, and many others needed access to these photos.

We are grateful to those who reviewed early versions of the book and offered feedback: University of Oregon Professor Emeritus Kenneth Helphand, former Portland Japanese Garden Curator of Culture Art and Education Diane Durston, and authors Lauren Glen Dunlap and Barbara Johns. Your thoughtful comments and encouragement were invaluable.

Over the past year, the collaborative efforts of many people brought this book to press.

Ellen Phillips-Angeles, Jason Wirth and the whole Kubota Garden editorial committee

Contributors

ANASTACIA-RENEÉ is the Civic Poet of Seattle and former 2015–2017 Poet-in-Residence at Hugo House. She is the author of *Forget It* (Black Radish Books, 2017), *(v.)* (Gramma Press, 2017), *Answer (Me)* (Argus Press, 2017), and *26* (Dancing Girl Press, 2016). Her poetry, prose, and fiction have been published widely.

BETSY ANDERSON is a park planner and landscape architect for Bellevue Parks & Community Services. She contributes to *Landscape Architecture Magazine* and previously served as a landscape architect for the National Park Service, working throughout the Western states. Her 2014 master's thesis for the University of Washington proposed a new vision for stormwater management in Dumbarton Oaks Park and received an ASLA Student Honor Award (General Design) and the Graduate School Distinguished Thesis Award. She was the first garden historian for The Mount, Edith Wharton's home in Massachusetts, and received a landscape history fellowship to write about the National Trust's Plant Conservation Programme in England and Northern Ireland.

ELIZABETH AUSTEN is a former Washington State Poet Laureate (2014–16), and the author of two chapbooks and a full-length collection, *Every Dress a Decision* (Blue Begonia Press, 2011). For the past decade she's led poetry/reflective writing workshops for healthcare providers, and for nearly twenty years was the on-air poetry correspondent for NPR-affiliate KUOW. She celebrated World Poetry Day at UNESCO in Paris, reading alongside a dozen poets from around the world. Elizabeth writes and gardens in West Seattle.

CLAUDIA CASTRO LUNA is Washington's current Poet Laureate and was Seattle's Civic Poet from 2015 to 2017. Her books include Pushcart-nominated *Killing Marías* (Two Sylvias Press) and *This City* (Floating Bridge Press). Born in El Salvador, Claudia came to the U.S. in 1981. A Hedgebrook and the Voices of our Nation Arts Foundation (VONA) alumna and a 2014 Jack Straw fellow, she has an MA in Urban Planning and an MFA in poetry. Her poems have appeared in Poetry Northwest, *La Bloga*, *Diálogo*, and *Psychological Perspectives*. Her nonfiction work is published in several anthologies, among them *This Is the Place: Women Writing About Home* (Seal Press).

JAMIE FORD is the great-grandson of Nevada mining pioneer, Min Chung, who emigrated from Kaiping, China to San Francisco in 1865, where he adopted the western name "Ford," thus confusing countless generations. His debut novel, *Hotel on the Corner of Bitter and Sweet*, spent two years on the *New York Times* bestseller list, went on to win the Asian/Pacific American Award for Literature, and has been optioned for film and stage. His second book, *Songs of Willow Frost*, was also a national bestseller. His work has been translated into 35 languages.

ALEX GALLO-BROWN is a poet, fiction writer, and essayist based in Seattle. He holds an MA in English from Georgia State University in Atlanta and a BFA in Creative Writing from the Pratt Institute in Brooklyn. He received an emerging artist award from WonderRoot and the City of Atlanta and has been published in the *Los Angeles Review of Books*, *The Brooklyn Rail*, *Salon.com*, *Literary Hub*, *The Stranger*, *Seattle Weekly*, *Poetry Northwest*, *Crosscut*, *The Oregonian*, *3:AM Magazine*, *Pacifica Literary Review*, *Seattle Review of Books*, *City Arts*, *Cirque*, *Cascadia Rising Review*, and *The Grief Diaries*, among others.

GEMINA GARLAND-LEWIS is a Seattle-based photographer, EcoHealth researcher, and National Geographic Explorer with experience in over 30 countries across six continents. She first picked up a camera when she was twelve years old and proceeded to spend the better part of high school in the darkroom in her hometown of Santa Fe, New Mexico. Both her photography and research explore the myriad connections between humans, animals, and their shared environments. In 2009 she spent several months in Japan and got her first taste of photographing traditional gardens. Two years later she moved to Seattle and began immersing herself in the landscapes of the Pacific Northwest. Though it took her seven years of living in the city before finding Kubota Garden, it quickly became a cherished space. Her photography and writing have been featured by *National Geographic News*, *National Geographic Adventure*, and REI, among others.

SAMUEL GREEN was named Washington's first poet laureate in December 2007. A thirty-year veteran of the Poetry-in-the- Schools program, Sam has taught in hundreds of classrooms. He served six terms as Distinguished Visiting Northwest Writer at Seattle University. His poems have appeared in numerous journals, including *Poetry*, *Poetry Northwest*, *Poet & Critic*, *Poetry East*, *Southern Poetry Review*, *Prairie Schooner*, and *Puerto del Sol*. Among his ten collections of poems are *Vertebrae: Poems 1972–1994* (Eastern Washington University Press, 1994) and *The Grace of Necessity* (Carnegie-Mellon University Press, 2008), which won the 2008 Washington State Book Award for Poetry.

JEFFREY HOU is a Professor in the University of Washington Department of Landscape Architecture. He focuses on community design, design activism, cross-cultural learning, and engaging marginalized communities in planning, design, and placemaking. Hou has written extensively on citizens' and communities' agency in shaping built environments, including *Transcultural Cities: Border-Crossing and Placemaking* (2013), *Now Urbanism: The Future City is Here* (2015), and *City Unsilenced: Urban Resistance and Public Space in the Age of Shrinking Democracy* (2017). Hou received the Places Book Award (2012, 2010), and Community Builder Award and Golden Circle Award for service in Seattle's Chinatown International District.

CHARLES JOHNSON is a novelist, essayist, literary scholar, philosopher, cartoonist, screenwriter, and professor emeritus at the University of Washington in Seattle. A MacArthur fellow, his fiction includes *Night Hawks*, *Dr. King's Refrigerator*, *Dreamer*, *Faith and the Good Thing*, and *Middle Passage*, for which he won the National Book Award. In 2002 he received the Arts and Letters Award in Literature from the American Academy of Arts and Letters. He lives in Seattle.

KENTARO KOJIMA is a stone sculptor. Born and raised in Guatemala, Kentaro graduated from the College of William and Mary. He was showroom and fabrication shop manager at Marenakos Rock Center, which has been connecting people with stone since the 1950s when Fujitarō Kubota's landscape business first sparked demand. Kentaro's articles have been published in the Japanese American newspaper *Hokubei Hochi* (North American Post Foundation) and on *Jungle City*, the Japanese/English website about all things Seattle.

SHANKAR NARAYAN is a three-time Pushcart Prize nominee, winner of the 2017 Flyway Sweet Corn Poetry Prize, and a former fellow at Kundiman and at Hugo House. He curates *Claiming Space*, a project to lift the voices of writers of color, and his chapbook, *Postcards from the New World,* won the Paper Nautilus Debut Series chapbook prize. Shankar draws strength from his global upbringing and from his work as a civil rights attorney for the ACLU. In Seattle, he awakens to the wonders of Cascadia every day, but his heart yearns east to his other hometown, Delhi.

GLENN NELSON is the founder of *The Trail Posse*, a media project about race and the outdoors. Born in Japan and raised in Seattle, Glenn graduated from Seattle University and Columbia University. He is the co-founder of the *Next 100 Coalition*, a national alliance of civil rights, environmental, and community groups advocating for more inclusive public land management. Formerly a writer for *The Seattle Times*, he's been published in numerous magazines and book collections. He's won several national awards for his writing, photography, and web publishing, most recently for Outstanding Beat Reporting (Race, Inclusion, and Environmental Justice) from the Society of Environmental Journalists.

SHIN YU PAI is an interdisciplinary artist and the author of several books including *ENSO* (Entre Rios Press, 2019), *AUX ARCS* (La Alameda, 2013), and *Adamantine* (White Pine, 2010). From 2015 to 2017, she served as the fourth poet laureate for the City of Redmond. Shin Yu has held residencies with Seattle Art Museum, Town Hall Seattle, and Jack Straw Cultural Center, and is a three-time fellow of The MacDowell Colony. She has received awards for her work from 4Culture, The Awesome Foundation, City of Seattle's Office of Arts & Culture, and Artist Trust.

IAIN ROBERTSON is an Associate Professor of Landscape Architecture at the University of Washington. He has a B.Arch. (Honours) from Edinburgh University, Scotland and an MLA from the University of Pennsylvania and is a registered landscape architect. Professor Robertson's professional interests focus on the spatial, functional, aesthetic, and ecological uses of plants in design and the role of creativity in the teaching and practice of design. He has completed plant-related projects in Washington Park Arboretum, the UW's Center for Urban Horticulture, and the Bloedel Reserve, and he has advised planning and design for arboreta in California and Arizona.

DAVID STREATFIELD is a preeminent historian of West Coast landscape architecture and is professor emeritus in the department of Landscape Architecture at the University of Washington, where he taught from 1971 to 2012 and served as department chair from 1992 to 1996. Streatfield was born and raised in England and received his Diploma in Architecture at Brighton College of the Arts and Crafts in 1956; he earned a Certificate in Landscape Architecture at University College, University of London, in 1962; and earned his Master of Landscape Architecture at the University of Pennsylvania in 1966. His book, *California Gardens: Creating a New Eden* (1994) was selected in 1998 by the American Horticultural Society as one of the "75 Great American Books in 75 Years" on the observance of the Society's 75th anniversary.

ANNA TAMURA is a landscape architect and planning portfolio manager for the Pacific West Region of the National Park Service. She coordinates development of planning portfolios for the more than sixty national parks in the Western states and Pacific Islands. Focusing on complex cultural landscapes and civil rights sites, she has managed several projects related to the World War II incarceration of Japanese Americans (Minidoka National Historic Site, Manzanar National Historic Site, Tule Lake Unit, Honouliuli National Monument, and the Bainbridge Island Japanese American Exclusion Memorial). A founding member of the annual Minidoka Pilgrimage, Tamura's family members were incarcerated at Minidoka and Tule Lake.

MAYUMI TSUTAKAWA is an independent writer and curator who focuses on Asian/Pacific American history and arts. Tsutakawa received her MA in Communications and her BA in East Asian Studies at the University of Washington. She co-edited *The Forbidden Stitch: Asian American Women's Literary Anthology,* which received the Before Columbus Foundation's American Book Award. She lives in Seattle.

THAÏSA WAY is an urban landscape historian teaching and researching history, theory, and design in the Department of Landscape Architecture at the University of Washington, Seattle. Her book *Unbounded Practice: Women, Landscape Architecture, and Early Twentieth Century Design* (University of Virginia Press, 2009) was awarded the J. B. Jackson Book Award in 2012. A second book, *From Modern Space to Urban Ecological Design: The Landscape Architecture of Richard Haag* (University of Washington Press, 2015) explores the narrative of post-industrial cities and the practice of landscape architecture. She has edited two books in urban environmental history and practice, including *Now Urbanism* (Routledge, 2013) with Jeff Hou, Ken Yocom, and Ben Spencer, and *River Cities/City Rivers* (Harvard University Press, 2018). She recently completed two monographs, *GGN Landscapes: 1998–2018* (Timber Press, 2018) and *Landscape Architect A. E. Bye: Sculpting the Earth,* Modern Landscape Design Series (Norton Publishing, forthcoming).

JASON M. WIRTH is a professor of philosophy at Seattle University, where he works and teaches in the areas of Buddhist philosophy, aesthetics, environmental philosophy, continental philosophy, and Africana philosophy. His recent books include *Mountains, Rivers, and the Great Earth: Reading Gary Snyder and Dōgen in an Age of Ecological Crisis* (SUNY Press, 2017); a monograph on Milan Kundera, *Commiserating with Devastated Things* (Fordham, 2015); *Schelling's Practice of the Wild* (SUNY Press, 2015); and the co-edited volumes *Japanese and Continental Philosophy: Conversations with the Kyoto School* (Indiana University Press, 2011) and *Engaging Dōgen's Zen* (Wisdom, 2016). He is the associate editor and book review editor of the journal *Comparative and Continental Philosophy*. He is an ordained priest in the Sōtō Zen lineage and co-director of the Seattle University EcoSangha. He is also a student in the Yabunōchi School of tea ceremony practice.

NATHAN WIRTH earned his BA and MA in English literature from San Francisco State University. Influenced by his continuing studies of poetry, painting, film, music, and the Japanese traditions of Zen, *karesansui*, bonsai, *ma*, *wabi-sabi*, ikebana, calligraphy, and *mushin*—he attempts to photograph silence. He teaches at City College of San Francisco and lives in Marin County, California, with his wife and daughter.

Index

Image Credits

Cover: Gemina Garland-Lewis

Cloth cover: Sean C. Malone

Back cover: Gemina Garland-Lewis

Page vi: Kubota Garden Foundation (KGF #575) Fujitarō Kubota in red pine, 1965

Page 8: Kubota Garden Foundation (KGF #39) Fujitarō Kubota at completed job site, Des Moines, Washington, 1970

Page 9: Gemina Garland-Lewis

Page 10: Gemina Garland-Lewis

Page 11: Kubota Garden Foundation (KGF #265) Fujitarō Kubota in the Garden, 1962; Josef Scaylea, photographer

Pages 12–13: Gemina Garland-Lewis

Page 14: Kubota Garden Foundation (KGF #103) Fujitarō Kubota in the Garden, 1960s

Page 17: Kubota Garden Foundation (KGF #2071) Fujitarō Kubota at Seattle University, 1965; Sean C. Malone, photographer

Page 18 (top left): Kubota Garden Foundation (KGF #181) Powell residence, 1968

Page 18 (top middle): Kubota Garden Foundation (KGF #108) Residential project, 1926

Page 18 (top right): Kubota Garden Foundation (KGF #106) Dunn Gardens, late 1920s

Page 18 (middle left): Kubota Garden Foundation (KGF #112) Residential project, late 1920s

Page 18 (center): Kubota Garden Foundation (KGF #127) Residential project, late 1920s

(middle right): Kubota Garden Foundation (KGF #398) Washington Federal Savings Bank, Bothell, Washington, 1963

Page 18 (bottom left): Kubota Garden Foundation (KGF #117) Madison Park (Seattle) residence, late 1920s

Page 18 (bottom middle): Kubota Garden Foundation (KGF #129) Capitol Hill (Seattle) residence, 1926

Page 18 (bottom right): Kubota Garden Foundation (KGF #110) May Kubota, residential project, 1926

Page 19: Malmo & Co. planting guide, 1924

Page 21: Kubota Garden Foundation (KGF #1957) Birch trees in the Garden, 1975; C. Dean Hodgson, photographer

Page 22: Kubota Garden Foundation (KGF #13) Kubota family and gardening crew; 1930s

Page 25: Kubota Garden Foundation (KGF #2112) Waterfall at Seattle University, 1965; Sean C. Malone, photographer

Page 26: Kubota Garden Foundation (KGF #91) Fujitarō Kubota on landscaping job, 1950s

Pages 30, 33, 34: Gemina Garland-Lewis

Page 36: Chris Kim

Page 37: Gemina Garland-Lewis

Page 41–42: Kubota Garden Foundation (KGF #1517) Fujitarō and Tom Kubota at Garden site, about 1930

Pages 43–47: Kubota Garden Foundation, various public sources

Page 48: Kubota Garden Foundation (KGF #4) Fujitarō Kubota and others at citizenship class, Broadway High School, 1955

Page 49: (KGF #5) Naturalization certificate, 1955

Page 50: Gemina Garland-Lewis

Page 53 (top left): Chris Kim

Page 53 (top right): Kubota Garden Foundation (KGF #349) Kubota Garden Foundation annual meeting, 1990

Page 53 (bottom left): Kubota Garden Foundation (KGF #361) Kubota Garden Foundation annual meeting, 1990

Page 53 (bottom right): Kubota Garden Foundation (KGF #974) Kubota Garden Foundation annual meeting, 1996

Page 54: Gemina Garland-Lewis

Page 57: Chris Kim

Pages 58–67: Gemina Garland-Lewis

Pages 68, 69: Joy Okazaki

Page 71 (top left, right, and bottom right): Antonia Angeles Hare

Page 71 (bottom left): Milt Footer

Page 72: Kubota Garden Foundation (KGF #47) Rockery along Renton Avenue, 1930s

Page 74: Kubota Garden Foundation (KGF #2085, #2082, #2986, #2988) Fujitarō placing stones at Seattle University, 1965; Sean C. Malone, photographer

Page 76: Chris Kim

Page 81, 82: Gemina Garland-Lewis

Pages 89–107: Nathan Wirth

Page 110, 113: (upper left, lower right): Gemina Garland-Lewis

Page 113 (upper right): Kubota Garden Foundation (KGF #1853) Entry gate dedication, 2004

Page 113 (bottom left): Kubota Garden Foundation (KGF #2296) Terrace Overlook dedication, 2015

Page 114: Kubota Garden Foundation (KGF #1542) Procession at Tak and Kiyo Kubota's wedding, 1940

Page 117 (left): Kubota Garden Foundation (KGF #1192) Prayer Stone, 1987

Page 117 (right): Kubota Garden Foundation (KGF #331) Prayer Stone, 1976

Page 118: Gemina Garland-Lewis

Pages 119, 120: Jason Wirth

Pages 121, 122: Gemina Garland-Lewis

Page 125: Konkō Church of Seattle

Colophon

This book was designed through the four seasons of 2019 in Seattle, Washington fueled by Cafe Allegro and a steady soundtrack of Kishi Bashi. The fonts are Chaparral for beauty, Avenir for simplicity, and Apoc for ornamentation.
· Kanji characters are in Hiragino Mincho.

Text pages are printed on Forest Stewardship Council (FSC) certified paper. The dust jacket is printed on 100# Coronado Stipple. The endsheets are Rainbow Fern. The cover cloth is screen printed and foil stamped Arrestox Pearl Grey.

FIRST EDITION OF 3,500 COPIES